Cromosys Publication

NIRANJAN JHA SHOWMAN

SPOKEN ENGLISH TOPICS

NIRANJAN JHA SHOWMAN

Founder - Niranjan Jha Showman

Education and Technology Research Center

Patankar Park, Nallasopara (W), Mumbai. +91-9561450045

Education, Technology, Publication, Healthcare, Newsmedia, Realtor, Filmmaking

www.facebook.com/cromosys

+91-9561450045
Learn Advanced Skills
And Get Job Instantly
GERMAN
Python
FRENCH
C++
SPANISH
Java
ENGLISH
HTML5
RUSSIAN
CSS
JavaScript
Cromosys
Education and Technology Research Center
Nallasopara (W), Mumbai

Learn Web Programming
Demo-Class Free
HTML
CSS
React
JavaScript
Typescript
Bootstrap
Cromosys
20 Years of Experience
Nallasopara (W), Mumbai
+91-9561450045

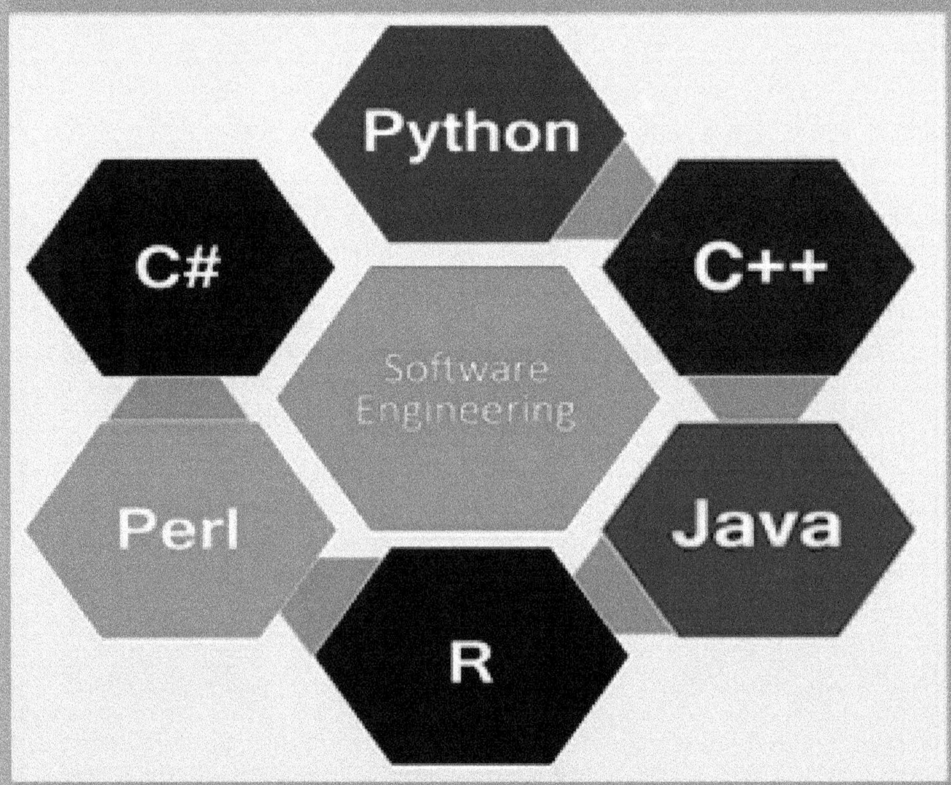
+91-9561450045
Learn Software Engineering
Demo-Class Free
Python
C#
C++
Software
Engineering
Perl
Java
R
Cromosys
20 Years of Experience
Nallasopara (W), Mumbai
+91-9561450045

25 Years of Experience
Learn Visual Multimedia
Animation VFX
Movie Editing
Game Development
Cromosys
+91-9561450045
Education and Technology Research Center
Nallasopara (W), Mumbai
www.facebook.com/cromosys

Jobs Available
For Candidates Who Know

German
French
Spanish

Vacancy in Germany, France, Spain

For Hospitality, Engineering, IT Sector
With Free Visa, Airfare and Accommodation

Cromosys
Education and Technology Research Centre
Nallasopara (W), Mumbai
+91-9561450045
20 Years of Experience

+91-9561450045
Foreign Languages Institute
German, French, Spanish
Basic and Advanced - All Levels
3 x 6 = 18 Courses
FRANCHISE
Business Offer
Teaching Materials Provided
We have 1 Million Students Globally
Great Income Assured
Global Exposure
Cromosys
20 Years of Experience
Nallasopara (W), Mumbai
+91-9561450045

Cromosys Publication

Spoken English Topics

Niranjan Jha Showman

"Education taken with zeal educes to success."
~Niranjan Showman

Preface

Cromosys Publication's "Spoken English Topics" book is an optimal quality guide to the beginners as well as advanced learners of English. This book teaches you all the common topics in detail that help you speak English, and become fluent as well as ultra-fluent in English. It starts with simple preformatted common topics of daily life, then several interesting stories, and then free-flow speaking topics. The lessons are so good, engaging and compelling that you automatically desire to speak. It is a proven track of becoming fluent in English as per our twenty-five years of record as languages trainers. And this book is equally useful for learners of all ages. This success-assured unique quality guide guarantees your improvement in speaking rapid, clear and correct English.

This "Spoken English Topics" books is to gain good knowledge of Spoken English by framing sentences fast and functional. The exclusive stories, topics and examples help you speak professionally in your interviews, at your corporate offices, and with foreigners of all over the world. It has well-explained lessons which are based on my fifteen years of research in linguistic field. The study materials are magnificently powerful to bring you into linguistic light. Since English is accepted as a global language, people around the world have been sharpening their knowledge to be good in it. Sometimes, only working knowledge of it doesn't work, and you feel that there is a lot more to explore. You feel that speaking slowly does not attract your listeners and you want to speak corporate level professional English. This is exactly for which this book prepares you.

The accurate and profound knowledge of this language, which was considered to be existing only in England and America in past, has influenced zillions of mind today. Therefore, I conceived the idea of making this book a guideline for those who want to be perfect in Written and Spoken English. The significance of this book is that it is dynamic, systemic and blissful with abundance of pure and perfect set of rules that took a decade of time in preparation. One being immaturely suggested, spend ages in reading literature, watching movies and listening to the audio, which help them to imitate a little but not learn what in actual sense it is. And their never-ending process of Picasso Adventure collects some scattered information which is unworthy to knowledge enhancement. So the aspirants get lost in wilderness.

Whether your intention is to travel abroad or plunge deep into your research, you have to be good in English to survive in today's world. After you start lessons of this book, you don't need to worry about anything but follow each and everything carefully. Don't procrastinate and never give up. You are going to do beautiful thing for yourself, so be bold and complete all the lessons. The sentence constructions explained in this book is the easiest method I could ever find and that need your practice with effort. The world growing with density has brought enormous opportunity to linguistic talents irrespective of their geographical boundaries. I strongly believe this book is useful for the people working for communication-based industry, media houses, entertainment world, and obviously for those who love English.

Cromosys, our education and technology research center, which is a path-breaking pioneer training institute for Spoken English, Foreign Languages, and Computer Science, is committed to enlightening human mind with educational endeavors, and we are doing the same from last successful twenty years. Having been teaching English and foreign languages from several years, I have come across numerous unique rules which I have elaborated and explained in this book. I believe I have done all that I could to make this book useful to you, and not only hopeful but I am sure that your success is in your hand now because this book will take you miles ahead in your expectation. We always respect the views and comments of readers, so for any communication with regards to assistance, enquiry or collaboration, we are always at your reach as it helps us improve our ability.

This fact may surprise you that almost seventy percent people of the world even today don't know how to speak proper English. And so, even in this 21st century, a large number of people are away from the benefits of communicating with native speakers. Whether you want to travel abroad or plunge deep into your research, your poor accent or bad pronunciation damages your reputation so much that neither a native speaker can understand you nor you can understand them. You may be very good in writing, but that is not enough today. With the growth of several multinational companies, there is a need of talented people to express clearly in the field of communication. The telecommunication industry has greatly inspired several people to have a good English accent so that the conversation takes place effectively. Being good in English accent and diction is a major advantage in getting a good job.

Niranjan Jha Showman
Trainer, Author Physician, Entrepreneur, Filmmaker, Activist
Founder - Cromosys Corporation
facebook.com/cromosys
+91-9561450045
cromosys@yahoo.com
Nallasopara (W), Mumbai, India

My other books: -
English Speaking and Grammar
English Word Power
English Voice Accent and Pronunciation
Teach Yourself German
Teach Yourself French
Teach Yourself Spanish
Be millionaire like me
Dynamic Grammar of English
Teach Yourself HTML5
Teach Yourself 3ds Max
Teach Yourself Autodesk Maya

Cromosys Corporation
Education and Technology Research Center
Education, Technology, Publication, Healthcare, Realtor, Filmmaking
facebook.com/cromosys
+91-9561450045
cromosys@yahoo.com
Nallasopara (W), Mumbai, India

About the Author

Niranjan Jha Showman
Trainer, Author, Physician, Entrepreneur, Filmmaker, Activist

Niranjan Jha Showman is a Language Scientist and Technical Researcher. He is the Award Winning author of more than fifty educational and fictional books at Amazon. He is one of the great-grandsons of the first President of India Dr. Rajendra Prasad. He is a Public Figure, and the globally - renowned Languages Trainer of French, Spanish, and German from past twenty years. Niranjan Jha Showman is an Entrepreneur and also works as a Filmmaker in India. Being the founder and owner of Cromosys Corporation - a company located in Mumbai, India, his company is excelling in the fields of Education, Technology, Publication, Newsmedia, Realtors, Banking, and Cinemascope from past fifteen years.

Niranjan Jha Showman's good-seller educational books and novels are appreciated worldwide. He has more than one million eBook buyers online, and more than one million learners are connected to him globally. One of his novels is critically acclaimed. He is the trainer of French, Spanish, German, English Voice and Accent, and Advanced Computer Education. He is also a political activist in India.

Niranjan Jha Showman is the man who came from rags to riches, he who knows how to turn the table, and he, whom you call the man of Midas-touch. He has observed lives from the Pandora of monkeys to the sanctuary of monks, not only down-to-earth but down-to-grave. He is a B. Com. graduate, and B. Ed. from Delhi University, and diploma holder in French, Spanish and German from America. You can watch his songs, movies, educational videos and many more things by typing "Niranjan Jha Showman" in Google.

Niranjan Jha Showman
+91-9561450045
cromosys@yahoo.com
Mumbai, India
facebook.com/cromosys

Statutory

This book with its content is the registered property of the author Niranjan Jha Showman.
The author and his Cromosys Publication holds all necessary rights of this book.
The copyright certificate of this book is attached at the end of this book.

Cromosys
Education and Technology Research Center

Spoken English Topics

+91-9561450045
Nallasopara (W), Mumbai
www.facebook.com/cromosys

Template Topics

You can change words as per your requirement.
Speak these topics in your classroom.
Also with friends, and then do video-recording.
While speaking, apply effective tone and emotion.

Topic 1
Self-Introduction

My name is ......
My father's name is ......
My education is ......
I am a ......
My ambition is to become a ......
I have ...... brothers and ...... sisters.
My father is a ...... (job).
And my mother is a ...... (job).
We stay at ......
My hobbies are ......
I always like ......
And I strongly dislike ......
There are total ...... members in my family.
We love each other very much.
My family is a happy family.
Thank you.

Topic 2
My Favorite Movie

The movie I like most is ......
I watched this movie in a ...... (theatre).
I watched it ...... years ago.
It was a nice experience for me.
It was in ...... language.
The hero of this movie is ......
And the heroine of this movie is ......
The story of this movie is very ......
The music is also ......
The best thing of this movie is ......
I watched it ...... times.
It is really a ...... movie.
I recommend it to all.
More detail about this movie is available online.
I would love to watch its sequel.
Thank you.

Speak these topics in classroom, then with friends, and then do video-recording.

Topic 3
My Favorite Actor

The actor I like most is ……
He / she is the actor of …… (Bollywood) film industry.
He is acting in movies from …… years.
I have watched his many movies.
The best movie of him is ……
I watched it …… years ago.
His acting in this movie is amazing.
He looks very handsome on the screen.
His speaking style is marvelous.
His other hit movies are ……
He is a great actor of film industry.
He is considered an A grade performer.
His movies are good in all sense.
He has millions of fan followers.
I am waiting for his next movie.
Thank you.

Topic 4
My Nice City

…… is a great city of India.
It is the …… (capital) of …… (state).
I have been living in this city for …… years.
This urban area is very populated.
People have busy life here.
This city is famous for ……
Living here is very expensive.
There are many beauty spots here like ……
My purpose of living here is ……
I like this city for its ……
We have good transport system.
I mostly travel by ……
The education system of this city is also helpful.
This is a city of global fame.
I wish all should know about it.
Thank you.

*You can change words as per your requirement.
Speak these topics in classroom, then with friends, and then do video-recording.

Topic 5
The Best Beauty Spot

The beauty spot I like most is ......
It is located at ......
It is one of the famous beauty spots of India.
I have visited this place ...... (five) times.
I came to know about it from ......
It is blissful and soul-soothing.
This place is known for ......
I like ...... of this spot very much.
The best time to visit it ......
Going by ...... (train) is most convenient for visitors.
It is also less expensive for people.
It takes .... of time for entire tour.
We see about this spot also on television.
Touring is always joyful to me.
I suggest all to visit this place once.
Thank you.

Topic 6
The Best TV Show

The best TV show for me is ......
It comes on ...... channel.
I have been watching this show for ...... years.
The schedule of this program is ...... (one hour).
This show is good for family entertainment.
Its presentation is also systematic.
The timing of it is ......
Watching television is a good jollification.
I like to watch ...... (comedy) part of this show.
It is coming on TV from past ...... years.
The best thing of this program is ......
It is an enjoyable show for all.
I don't miss any part of this program.
People of all age love to watch this show.
This show is very famous among urban people.
Thank you.

Speak these topics in classroom, then with friends, and then do video-recording.

Topic 7
My Favorite Brand

The brand name I like most is ......
I use ...... product of this brand.
I have been using it for ...... years.
Its name also looks good to me.
The quality of this brand is ...... (good).
I purchase its product for ...... rupees.
These products are worth the price.
My family also uses this product.
This brand company originated in ...... (India).
The best thing of this brand is ......
The other products of this brand are ....
These products are available all over.
I came to know about it from ......
Their advertisement is also seen everywhere.
I recommend this brand to all.
Thank you.

Topic 8
My Favorite Newspaper

The newspaper I like most is ......
It is a daily newspaper.
It is published in ...... language.
I have been reading this for ...... years.
Newspaper reading is good for knowledge.
I like to read ...... (editorial) part of his paper.
My family also likes this newspaper.
The price of it is ...... rupees.
It is also available on the Internet.
The best thing of this paper is ......
I read it regularly in morning.
We learn a lot from its language.
It has well-organized presentation.
Its language is easy and effective.
Is suggest others to read this this newspaper.
Thank you.

Speak these topics in classroom, then with friends, and then do video-recording.

Topic 9
My Ideal Person

My ideal person is ......
He / she was born in ......
I like ...... quality of him a lot.
I came to know about him from ......
He is known to all for his ...... (quality).
I learnt from him to progress in life.
He really deserves to be called my ideal.
I also recollect his advices in difficult time.
He is a good motivator for my life.
We can find more information about him from ......
People talk about his achievement quite often.
He shaped my career and life.
He is the most inspirational person for me.
We love to talk about his persona.
I want all should know about him.
Thank you.

Topic 10
Learning at Cromosys

Cromosys is an education and technology research center.
It is located a Nallasopara West in Mumbai.
I am learning ...... from Cromosys.
I have opted for ...... months of course.
Learning this course is needful for my career.
It will help me for a good job.
I came to know about Cromosys from ......
This education center is teaching this course from ......
My trainer's name is ......
My experience of learning here is ......
The special element of education here is ......
Cromosys originated in Mumbai.
This academic enter has ...... years of experience.
It also teaches other courses such as ....
It recommend it to my all acquaintants.
Thank you.

Speak these topics in classroom, then with friends, and then do video-recording.

Story Speaking

You can make short changes if required.
Speak these stories in your classroom.
Also with friends, and then do video-recording.
While speaking, apply effective tone and emotion.
Use correct pronunciation and good accent and diction.

Story 1
The Bread Seller

Once there was a bread seller in a city. He was well experienced and his breads were very tasty. He used to sell breads at the price of Rs. 5 each from a long time. Considering no profit in the business, he wanted to increase the price up to Rs. 10. For this, he goes to the king for permission. The king orders him to make it Rs. 30 per bread. The bread seller says surprisingly: Your majesty, there will be chaos in public. The king say: Let it be. You do what I said.

Next day, a lot of people come to the king and complain about the bread seller. The king sends his soldiers to arrest him as soon as possible. When he is brought into the place, the king says dramatically: You wicked, why you didn't ask me before increasing the price? Do you want to let our people die? Before the bread seller says anything, the king orders: From tomorrow, the price will Rs. 15 per bread. Hearing this, all people get happy and start praising the king. And the king smiles at the bread seller cleverly.

Story 2
The Old Clock

There was a roadside clock shop in London. Every morning and evening people passed through the way. One day an old man comes in front of the shop, he stops for a minute, does something and goes away. As it is the first day, so the shopkeeper doesn't notice. The next day again the old man comes and does the same. By the time the shopkeeper wants to talk, the man is already gone. So the next day, the shopkeeper comes out and starts waiting for him.

When he comes, he asks, "Uncle, I'm the owner of this shop. I see that you do here something every day. May I know what you do?" The uncle says, "My son, I work as a security guard for this nearby company. My job is to blow siren at 5 pm. Then the labors go home. But as I am old, my watch is also old, and loses time every night. So I look at your big clock and set the time of my watch." Hearing this, the shopkeeper starts laughing. The uncle asks, "I told you the truth, now why are you laughing?" The shopkeeper says, "Uncle, this big clock is also very old and loses time every day. So when I hear your siren at 5 pm, I set the time of this clock every day.

With your own addition and style, speak these stories in classroom without seeing notebooks. You can also speak with friends and do video-recording. Apply effective tone, emotion, correct pronunciation, good accent and diction.

Story 3
Nothing Right Nothing Wrong

A religious seminar was organized in Chicago city of America. The priests of all religions were invited to attend the seminar. In the morning, they start speeches. And in the afternoon, they come to the dining hall for lunch. The first priest standing in the queue was father William. And behind him was mullah Nasiruddin. Father William takes a plate in his hand and gives another to mullah Nasiruddin. Now William takes some rice and gives some to Nasiruddin.

Now he takes pork, and offers the same to Mullahji. But Mullahji denies and says that pork is a dirty food in his religion. The father says: How can pork be dirty? Mullahji, if you haven't eaten pork, you haven't enjoyed the taste of food. Mullahji says: Don't worry father, we have some other dishes. As they move ahead, now Mullahji enquires: Father, who cooks food for you? He replies: I have a maid. Mullahji asks: Does your wife not cook for you? Father says: We are Christian priests, so we don't get married. Mullahji exclaims with surprise: Father William, get married, because marriage is tastier than pork.

Story 4
LIC Unemployment

Once there was a man in Delhi and he was jobless from a long time. As his financial condition was not good, so his friends suggested him to visit an LIC office and ask for a job. Next day he goes there and meets the manager. He says that he is a graduate and looking for a job. The manager replies: Sorry, we are already over-staffed. At present we have no vacancy, if we have one, we'll let you know. Now he leaves for home and decides to walk on foot because of no money.

While walking over the Yamuna Bridge, he sees a man drowning into the water. He wants to save the man, so he rushes down and tries to pull the man out of water. By the time he brings him out, the man was already dead. Looking at the dead man's identity card, he finds that he was working for the same LIC office where he was coming from. He leaves the dead body there runs towards the same office. He tells the manager that while he was going home, he found an LIC personnel drowning into Yamuna and subsequently he was dead. And now as he is already dead, so there should be one vacancy in the office. The manager replies firmly: Sorry dear, you're late. The man who pushed him into the river came before you and took the job away.

With your own addition and style, speak these stories in classroom without seeing notebooks. You can also speak with friends and do video-recording. Apply effective tone, emotion, correct pronunciation, good accent and diction.

Story 5
Indian Politician

Let's talk about man of Delhi named Dhaniram. He had a son and he was anxious about his future. When he asks a punditji about his son's future, and he advises to send his son abroad for education. Obeying the punditji, Dhaniram sends his son for ten years of study. After ten years, tomorrow his son is returning India. So today he goes to the punditji again. Now the punditji says: To know the future of your son, you place four things on a table in a room. A wine bottle, a revolver, some money, and some hot pictures. If your son picks up the bottle, he will become a drinker, if revolver then a criminal, if money then a business, and if pictures then a filmstar.

Dhaniram places all four things and starts waiting for his son. When his son comes, he takes the bottle and starts drinking, takes the revolver and put into his pocket, takes the money and kisses the pictures. Feeling shocked, without meeting his son, he rushes to the punditji and explains him the situation. The punditji says: Don't worry Dhaniram, if your son took all four things together that means he will become an Indian politician.

Story 6
Language Gap

A young man named Sibu lived in Kerala. He joins a Christian missionary and becomes the member of a group of ten people. Their leader takes them to Jharkhand for social service and publicizing Christianity among tribal people. The entire group along with Sibu knew only Malayalam language, and only the leader knew both Hindi and Malayalam. It was a hot summer day when they enter a tribal village. The leader starts explaining about Christianity and the entire group assist them.

When it was afternoon, the leader tell the group members that he would go to the church to bring food for them. By that time, they have to sit under the tree, and not to talk to anyone because not knowing Hindi language at all. After he leaves, Sibu feels thirsty and he wishes to ask for a glass for water from the villager. He enters a house but finds no response. When he goes deep inside, a strongman asks him in Hindi: Kya tum chor ho? For Sibu, the word 'chor' in Malayalam – 'rice'. So he said: Yes. The strongman repeated the same question and he replied with the same answer. The man starts beating Sibu and then the entire group because no one knew Hindi. After several minutes, the leader comes running from the church and tells the strongman to stop. He explains that there was a problem because of language gap.

With your own addition and style, speak these stories in classroom without seeing notebooks. You can also speak with friends and do video-recording. Apply effective tone, emotion, correct pronunciation, good accent and diction.

Story 7
The Father and the Donkey

Once there lived a man in a village. He had a son and a donkey. One day he decides to go to market and tells his son to get ready. When the son is ready, he situates him on the donkey and he himself starts walking on foot. At some distance on the way, some people look at them and comment: See, how shameless the child is! He is enjoying on the donkey and his old father is walking behind. Now the child says: Father, people are commenting on us, you sit on the donkey and I will walk behind. Now the father sits on the donkey.

At some distance again some people look and comment: See, how careless the father is! He is enjoying on the donkey and his small child is walking behind. Now the father says: Son, people are commenting, so we both should sit on the donkey. As they both sit, again at some distance people comment: See, how cruel the father and the son is! They are enjoying and the poor donkey is dying in pain. Now the father says: No, this is also not right. People are still commenting on us, so we would take donkey on our shoulder. They tie the donkey's legs, and with the help of a bamboo, they took on their shoulders. But before reaching the market, they had to cross a bridge, and the donkey seeing water shakes its body. Finally, it falls into the river.

Story 8
Chhedilal

This is the story of a man of Delhi whose name was Chhedilal. People used to call him 'Chhedi' and he hated this name a lot. He wanted to change his name but had no knowledge. One day, some of his friends give him an advice. They suggest him to change his religion so that his name would automatically change. Next day, Chhedilal goes to a mosque and asks mullaji to change his religion. After the paperwork completes, mullaji asks his previous name. He replies: Chhedilal. Now mullaji says: As your name was Chhedilal, so now in Islam religion your name will be 'Surakh Khan'. And Chhedilal hates this name too.

Now he goes to a church and asks the father to change his religion. After the paperwork completes, father asks his previous name. He replies: Surakh Khan. Now father says: As your name was Surakh Khan, so now in Christianity your name will be 'Mister Hole'. And Chhedilal hates this name too. At last he attempts to go to a gurudwara and asks gyaniji to change his religion. After the paperwork completes, the gyaniji asks his previous name. He replies: Mister Hole. Now gyaniji says: As your name was Mister Hole, so now in Sikhism your name will be 'Gaddha Singh'. And Chhedilal bluntly replies: You keep this name for yourself, I go back to become Chhedilal again.

With your own addition and style, speak these stories in classroom without seeing notebooks. You can also speak with friends and do video-recording. Apply effective tone, emotion, correct pronunciation, good accent and diction.

Story 9
Afternoon Darkness

There was a writer in London and one day he was taking a morning walk on the hills. Suddenly a storm comes and he falls down. While rolling down, he comes into the valley, and loses the direction to go back home. At some distance into the valley, he only sees some huts. As the writer gets in, he sees an old man sitting inside. He says: Sir, I am from the city and I fell down here because of the storm. Could you tell me how to go back to my house? The old man says: City… House… I haven't heard these words before. Perhaps you are dreaming, so you can go to sleep. But the old man's daughter was listening, so she says to her father: Perhaps this stranger is saying something true. Can we help him in any manner?

The old man replies: Yes, we'll take him to our doctor. As they come out, the writer notices that it was a hamlet of all blind people, so the doctor was also blind. Upon reaching the doctor, the old man says: This stranger came to me this morning looking for his city and house. As I don't know anything about it, so can you please check what the problem with him is? The doctor examine his body and replies: Uncle, I find two organs above his nose and below forehead. If I remove them, he will be like us and will not talk anything irrelevant. Hearing this, the writer takes his steps back and starts running. In fear, he crosses two hills, and then sits down with closed eyes because of tiredness. When he opens eyes, he sees his own city… his own house.

Story 10
Keep the Fire Burning

A crew of Discovery channel enters a forest in Mexico. As they go deep inside, they observe something unusual. They see some smokes coming from somewhere as it appeared man-made and not natural. Following the direction of the smoke and ready with video-shooting, they reach the exact spot. Now they see some tribal sitting in a circle around the fire. They were putting coals in fire to keep it burning.

After great efforts, the crew members succeed in asking them reason of sitting there. They said in their language that their ancestors had invented fire. But the next generation forgot to create fire. So they found some fire at some place, brought them here, and they sit to guard the fire and keep it burning since ages. And they have no hope of fire being found anywhere else. Feeling perplexed, the crew members bring some of the tribal out of forest. The jungly people, after coming out feel astonished seeing how much humans have done with fire in new world!

Story 11
The Chilly Boy

This is the story of a naughty boy of Mumbai. He was very persistent by nature. One day he insists upon eating a chilly. His parents forbid him and explain the bad effect of chilly but he still insists. They decide to call his teacher to make their child understand the bad consequence. The teacher also explains a lot but the naughty boy fails him too. So the teacher says: OK, let him eat a chilly. Thus he brings a chilly to him.

Now the boy says: I want to eat the fried one. The teacher gets it fried and tells him to eat. Looking at him carefully, the boy says: I want to eat half of it. The teacher exclaims: OK, that's a good idea! He cuts the chilly in two halves and now persuades him to eat. The boy, master in mischief, now says: No, you eat the first half, then I will eat. In extreme puzzlement, quite hesitatingly, the teachers eats the one half and tells him to eat the next half. Now the boy says: Oh my God, you ate the first half that I wanted to eat. Now I will not eat.

Story 12
Bhelpuri

Once there was a bhelpuri shop at a good location in Mumbai. People all around the locality liked this shop because of its good taste. It had a menu card hanging in front with items written in bold letters. One day, in the evening time, a customer enters the shop for the first time. He wants to read the menu before ordering bhelpuri. It reads: Regular bhelpuri - Rs. 20, Special bhelpuri – Rs. 30, and Super bhelpuri – Rs. 40. The customer asks the owner: What's the difference among these three kinds of bhelpuri?

The owner smiles at him and replies: Regular is just normal one. Then the customer asks curiously: What is the special one? He responds: Special one is served in washed plate and spoon. The customer feels astonished and has no word in mouth. After a little effort, he tries to ask: Then what is the super one? The owner says: It is available only on Sunday. The customer asks: Why? The owner gives bewildering answer: Because I take bath only on Sunday.

With your own addition and style, speak these stories in classroom without seeing notebooks. You can also speak with friends and do video-recording. Apply effective tone, emotion, correct pronunciation, good accent and diction.

Story 13
Dr. Jack and Mr. Hide

Dr. Jack was a very famous physician in Australia. One day, after long research, he invents a medicine that makes a good person bad, and a bad person good. Before giving it out for public use, he wants to try on himself. Dr. Jack prepares two glasses of medicine in night, drinks one and he becomes bad. Then he takes a rod in hand, goes out in dark streets, and starts beating people vehemently. All berserk, he comes home, drinks the second glass and becomes good. And nobody suspects him. But now he gets addicted to it.

Then next day, and every day, he continues beating people in night and gains the name as Mr. Hide. It becomes his habit and he enjoys tremendously. One day, being in a hurry, he prepares only one glass of medicine instead of two. He forgets to prepare the second glass, drinks the first glass, and goes out to beat people. After an hour, when he comes home and looks for the second glass, he finds nowhere. As he had become bad, he didn't know how to prepare the second glass. In exasperation, Mr. Hide cries and starts beating his head against the wall. And after a while, he dies with bleeding head.

Story 14
Alcoholic

Punjab had fallen badly in liquor addiction. A lot of social activities were going on to make people aware of the bad effect of liquor. One day, a doctor is called in a college to demonstrate about the harmfulness of alcohol. Among a big audience, he goes to the stage and puts two glasses on a table. He fills one with distilled water, and the second with liquor. Then he puts an earthworm in the first glass and let the audience see. Now the doctor puts the same earthworm in the second glass. The worm dies instantly.

He lets the viewers see the glass with dead worm. Now he probes: So have you all understood how liquor can affect our body? One among the audience responds: Yes, if we drink liquor, it will kill all worms of stomach. The doctor gets angry on the wrong perception of the viewers. In the second demonstration, he brings a donkey on the stage and lets it drink liquor. As the donkey does not drink, so he asks firmly: Now do you all see? Another one replies: Yes, who doesn't drink liquor is a donkey.

With your own addition and style, speak these stories in classroom without seeing notebooks. You can also speak with friends and do video-recording. Apply effective tone, emotion, correct pronunciation, good accent and diction.

Story 15
Yadav Ji

Once there was a village full of Brahmin families. But it had one Yadav family living in the middle. Yadav ji cooked chicken quite often and the smell went around to the Brahmins living in the neighborhood. The Brahmins wanted to get rid of this problem but didn't know how. One day they call a meeting and come up with a plan. They decide to make Yadav ji a Brahmin, and regarding this, they also take the approval of their senior priest. Next week, the Brahmins take Yadav ji to the biggest temple for accepting Brahmanism.

In the temple, the senior priest pours gangajal on him and pronounces: You were born as Yadav, but from today, you are a Brahmin. Yadav ji comes home after accepting Brahmanism. But from next day, the smell of chicken starts coming from his again. The neighbors gather around his house stealthily and want to peep inside through a window. They find that Yadav ji is cooking chicken. But they also see that he is pouring gangajal on the chickens and saying: You were born as chickens, but from today, you are potatoes.

Story 16
The Telephone Lineman

There was a manager in an office and he had the nature of dominating over his staffs. One day he brings a calendar in his office and hangs on the wall. The calendar reads: I'm your boss, you have to follow me. In evening, his wife comes to the office when he was in meeting. She enters the meeting room and asks: Give me my calendar back. Feeling ashamed, the manager gives the calendar to his wife. When the owner of the company comes to know about his nature, he transfers him to a different branch.

Sitting in his new cabin of the first day in morning, the manager hears a knock at the door. He wants to impress the visitor, and so he picks up the receiver of his phone. He starts boasting about big financial transactions on the phone. By the time, the visitor gets in and stands near his table in waiting. Now he puts down the receiver and asks the visitor what brings him here? The receiver says: I'm a telephone lineman, and I am here to connect your phone to the line.

With your own addition and style, speak these stories in classroom without seeing notebooks. You can also speak with friends and do video-recording. Apply effective tone, emotion, correct pronunciation, good accent and diction.

Story 17
Alif Laila

A long time ago, Arabia was ruled by a king. The king had a beautiful and beloved wife, but after some years of marriage, his wife died. In the bereavement of his wife, he gets succumbed to upset life. Many of his sympathizers advise him for remarriage, but he rejects. With passing time, his mindset changes and he gets ready for marriage. He marries a girl, and being fond of listening to stories, he tells his new wife to narrate him one. As she finishes the story, he kills her. And the next day he says that he wants to marry again.

Next day he marries again, and kills his wife after she finishes the story. Now everyday he commits the same crime. This way, he had decided to kill all women of Arabia. One day, the daughter of the king's minister decides to marry him. Her father forbids but she says that the king must be stopped. Otherwise there will be no girl left in the country. She marries the king next day and starts narrating a story on his request in night. But the story doesn't end even till early morning. The kings allows her to continue the same story next night. And this way, she continues the story for months. And with passing time, the king falls in love with her.

Story 18
The Twist of Blessing

A youngster named Buddhudev lived in Nepal. Born as feeble minded, he was not able to decide what to do in life. Some of his friends suggested him to meditate upon God. He finds a forest and starts meditation. After some months pass, God comes to know about his meditation and comes to fulfill his wishes. He says: Buddhudev, I'm happy to see your meditation. And I want to fulfill your three wishes. Buddhudev opens his eyes and sees God in front.

He says: God, if you want to fulfill my three wishes, then my first wish is that — if a go to a tailor for stitching, he shouldn't steal a single inch of my cloth. God says: Amen! Now your second wish! Buddhudev says: If I go to a sweet-seller, he shouldn't steal sweet while weighing. God says: Amen! Now your last wish! Buddhudev says: My third wish is that whenever I want, I can ask for another three wishes. God says 'Amen', but he also understands that there is a big twist in it. After a week, Buddhudev goes on a pilgrimage, and he feels thirsty in the way. He calls God and asks for a watermelon as his first wish. God says: I want to take you to a place where there are lots of watermelon. And even whatever you wish, you will get there. Will you come with me? As Buddhudev agrees, God takes him to heaven.

Story 19
The Cyber Cafe

Once in the afternoon, a teenager enters a cyber cafe. He tells the owner that he wants to email a love letter to his girlfriend. He leaves after emailing. But an hour later, he returns and says to the owner: I think my girlfriend's sister is also beautiful. That's why I want to email her a love letter too. After sending both of emails, he leaves for his girlfriend's house. He reaches late in evening and gets engaged in long conversation with both of his female friends.

The long conversation makes dinner time to come and they prepare food for him. After cooking, as soon as the food is served on the table, her father enters. He barely looks at her father and bends down his head for prayer to the meal. But the prayer seems to be going long and he is not lifting up head. Now his girlfriend wants to interrupt, so she remarks surprisingly: I didn't know that you are so religious! The nervous boy, still bending head, whispers into her ears: I didn't know that your father runs a cyber cafe.

Story 20
Thieves Market

A man in Mumbai lost a wheel cover of his beautiful car. He visits many mechanics for the same kind of cover but doesn't find. Finally, looking at his new car, some advise him to go to thieves market and try there. Next day, he reaches the market and stops at an automobile shop. He asks the repairists for the same wheel over which other three wheels of his car had. By that time, the shopkeeper approaches him and agrees for the availability. The car owner is offered tea and told to wait for ten minutes.

He starts taking tea, and after ten minutes, two repairists of the shop come up with the same cover. He feels exultant, pays 1000 rupees and leaves for home giving them a good gesture. As it was late in evening, so he decides to go to his mechanic in morning. In morning, when the mechanic wants to fix the cover, he finds that one more wheel has lost the cover. So now, total two wheels were without cover. The owner gets perplexed, and rushes to the thieves market. When he asks the shopkeeper, he totally denies from recognizing him.

With your own addition and style, speak these stories in classroom without seeing notebooks. You can also speak with friends and do video-recording. Apply effective tone, emotion, correct pronunciation, good accent and diction.

Story 21
Love You My Husband

A few years ago, a woman welfare association in Mumbai organized a program for married women. Some media personnel were also invited to telecast this show live. It was an effort to check love between husbands and wives who have busy lives in cities and get less time to communicate. They call almost fifty women to participate in the competition. They ask the participants to send an "I love you" message to their husbands and show the reply. The best reply is to win an exciting prize.

Almost fifty women send the message from their cellphones to husbands. After sometime, they start getting replies. The receiving messages are being shown on a big screen so that all can see. One gets the reply: You got fever again? Go and have some pills. The second gets the reply: I have told you to not watch horror movies, but you don't listen. But the woman who wins the prize, she gets very exhilarating response. Her husband replies: "Who?"

Story 22
Contraceptive Pills

There were three fools talking to each other. One by one, each was claiming that his wife was the biggest fool in the world. In order to prove, the first one speaks: In last festival, my wife bought 10 kg of sweets, she could barely eat 1 kg, and rest was given to neighbors. On this, the second fool speaks: This is nothing. I tell you about my wife. She bought a car last month without knowing driving. Now the car is in garage.

The third fool was listening to both of them. Now he utters: No, there is nothing serious in them. My wife is the biggest fool in the world and I can prove it. Last month she was going to Goa for a trip alone. While packing the luggage, she took some contraceptive pills along. What was the use of them when she was going alone? And both of them laughs at him agreeing that his wife is the biggest fool in the world.

Story 23
The Parliamentarian

There was a parliamentarian in India. He had won last election with major votes, and so he was planning for the next. With the next election round the corner, he intends to visit some remote areas of his parliamentary constituency. At first, the MP plans to visit a flood-affected village. But before reaching the village, his personal assistant warns him with a piece of information. And he says: Sir, the flood water here is flowing above the danger mark. What should we do? The MP orders: Raise the danger sign above.

Not being able to do anything for the flood, the politician enters the village. As he reaches the residents, he asks an old man: What are the other problems here except the one I just resolved? An old man says: There are two problems in this village. The first is that there is no doctor here. The MP makes a call from his cellphone, and says: "Done." What is the second problem? The old man replies: There is no mobile network here.

Story 24
An Antique Bowl (boal)

There lived a grocer in a town and he had a cat. The cat used to drink milk from an antique bowl. One day an antiquarian was passing through the way and he stops at the grocery shop. He was a good antique dealer over the years. The reason he stopped was the bowl from which the cat was drinking milk. He familiarizes himself with the grocer. Then he tells: Lalaji, I want to buy your beautiful cat. Tell me the price please.

After much bargain, the cat's price is fixed ten thousand rupees. He pays the money in cast. As he buys the cat and moves ahead, he turns back to the grocer smilingly. "You have sold your cat, so give me the bowl also," the antiquarian requests. The grocer responds: No, I won't. The dealer makes him understand that now he has no use of the bowl. But he finally reveals: Because of this bowl, I've sold fifty cats.

With your own addition and style, speak these stories in classroom without seeing notebooks. You can also speak with friends and do video-recording. Apply effective tone, emotion, correct pronunciation, good accent and diction.

Story 25
The Tomb (toom)

There was a tomb in a village in Pakistan that was worshiped devotionally by every passerby. A cloth seller named Suleman came and took rest there daily. One day, Suleman looks very worried, and the caretaker of the tomb named Musa asks him the problem. He says that with passing age, he is unable to bear the load of cloths daily. Taking pity on him, Musa gives Suleman a donkey to sell cloths far and wide.

But one day, the donkey dies on the way. He buries and starts crying there. The passerby, seeing a grave and a man crying, start worship the place. And this way, with the gradual increase of crowd as worshipers, Suleman becomes the caretaker of this tomb. Knowing popularity of this new tomb, Musa comes to visit and sees Suleman there as the caretaker. He says to Musa: It all happened because his donkey died there. Now Musa replies: The first tomb that I manage is the grave of this donkey's mother.

Story 26
The Egg Seller

Let's talk about an egg seller. His duty was to carry and sell eggs on a bicycle. One day, while riding the bicycle in morning, he hits a wall and all of his eggs get broken. People approach and comment about the dirty smell. Suddenly from the crowd, an uncle appears and says: Leave this matter aside, and think, what will his owner tell him? He will cut money from his salary. So we should do something for him to compensate his loss.

While saying this, the uncle drops ten rupees there with kindness. Now other people also start giving money, and gradually, almost all contribute some amount. After a while, the money becomes more than the eggs' value. The seller collects all the money and prepares to leave the place. But one person appears from behind with a question. He asks: By the way, who is your owner? And the seller replies: The same uncle!

With your own addition and style, speak these stories in classroom without seeing notebooks. You can also speak with friends and do video-recording. Apply effective tone, emotion, correct pronunciation, good accent and diction.

Story 27
The Blanket

This is the story of a district magistrate who had a beautiful house in a city. Every morning, he had the habit of observing people moving through the road. One morning, as he opens the window, he sees a beggar shivering in cold at the road. Seeing him in a pitiful condition, the magistrate orders his assistant to give him a blanket today. Then he leaves for the office and returns late in night. Next morning, he sees the beggar in same condition without a blanket.

When he asks, the assistant replies: If we give him a blanket, we have to give to all the beggars. So today, we will buy and give blankets to all. Next day in morning, the magistrate sees the beggar dead without a blanket. Now the assistant replies: Sir we were giving blankets to all, so we arranged their names alphabetically, but his name started with Z letter. Meanwhile, some fake beggars entered the queue, and by the time his turn came, we had no blanket.

Story 28
Mirror Effect

An African, while moving in a forest, gets a piece of glass. Before this he hadn't seen any glass so he got attracted to it. He brings the piece home and looks into it. He sees a face inside, and assumes, that is his father. Now he starts talking to face almost every day. One day, his wife notices his talking activity and wants to investigate. When the man is out for some work, she picks up the mirror in hand and sees a face inside.

Her doubt increases and she believes this is the woman her husband talks to so often. Getting angry, she comes to her mother-in-law with the complaint. She speaks: Your son looks into this piece and talks to this woman quite frequently. The mother takes the piece in her hand to observe. She also finds a face inside but replies: You are right but you don't need to worry. This woman is very old and will die soon!

With your own addition and style, speak these stories in classroom without seeing notebooks. You can also speak with friends and do video-recording. Apply effective tone, emotion, correct pronunciation, good accent and diction.

Story 29
The Treasure Key

There was a wealthy man living in a town who had an obedient servant. One day, the man sends his servant to market for buying liquor. But he returns empty handed and replies: Seth ji, the shop was closed today. The seth comments with disbelief and the servant responds: You have to believe because today is a dry day. The rich man understands the fact. The servant proves his honesty but he had to settle one more matter with the seth.

Now he verbalizes: Seth ji, the problem is that you never trust me. The seth disagrees but he still continues: You really don't trust me, so I want to leave this job. The seth gets afraid and doesn't want to lose the obedient servant. Now he enquires: How can you say that? Don't you know that I have given you my treasure key? The servant, without wasting a second answers quickly: But the fact is that the key never opens your treasure!

Story 30
The Horse Flyer

A king comes to know that some gold from his palace has been stolen recently. The soldiers find the thief and bring him to the king. He asks angrily: Who gave you the tip to enter my palace? The thief replies: Your minister, and he took his share from me. But the king rejects by saying: You are lying and there is no gold with my minister. The king gives him death punishment and asks his last wish before death.

The thief replies that he wants to show him the trick of flying a horse. The king feels amazed and gives him a horse to fly. The thief, knowing nothing about flying a horse, had succeeded in speculation. Now he asks some time to train the horse and takes a period of three years. The time begins to pass, but in third year something strange happens. A king from different empire attacks his king. And the thief gets free forever.

Story 31
Share Market

A businessman goes to a village with his assistant. He says to the villagers that he wants to buy monkeys for one thousand rupees each. All the villagers catch monkeys and sell to the businessman. Now this trend slows, so he goes to the villagers again and announces: I want more monkeys and now the price is two thousand rupees each. They try hard, catch some more and sell to him. When this trend also slows, the business goes to the villagers again with big offer: I really want some more monkeys and this time the prices is ten thousand rupees each. And then, he leaves the village.

Now there was no monkey in forest, so they come empty to the assistant who was in the office. When they tell the problem, the assistant advises: you buy these monkeys for five thousand rupees each, as the boss is not here. When he comes next week, you can sell them to him for ten thousand. This way, they bought up all the monkeys from the assistant. But next week, they find no office, no assistant – only monkeys. This is what happens in share marketing.

Story 32
The Earth is Round

Once there was a king in a territory who was very generous to the public. Learning about his prominence, a hermit comes to his court with an immortalizing apple. He gives the apple to the king telling him that that will make him immortal. But the king adored his queen tremendously, so he gives the apple to her considering her worthy to live forever. However the queen had a lover, so she thought he should live forever instead of her.

And she gives the fruit to him as a gift from her side. But then lover visited a prostitute, so he gives the apple to her against some dues that he was unable to pay. Now the prostitute, looking at the apple in hand, doesn't feel worthy to live same life eternally. She thinks her king is the right person to eat this apple and be immortal. Next day, the prostitute comes to the king's court and gives the same apple to him.

With your own addition and style, speak these stories in classroom without seeing notebooks. You can also speak with friends and do video-recording. Apply effective tone, emotion, correct pronunciation, good accent and diction.

Story 33
The Accident

A man was driving a car on a highway. And suddenly, his car is hit by another car coming from opposite side. He sees that that car was being driven by a woman. Seeing her, and also his vehicle completely damaged, she expresses: God saved both of us, so we should become friends. The man nodded, and she still continues: See the wine bottle in my car is still safe. I think we should have some. And the man agrees.

He wants to have some wine offered by the beautiful woman at the desolate place. He takes some sips gives the bottle to her to have. But the woman caps the bottle without drinking and states: I call the police because you are drunk and you hit my car. At first, it comes shocking to him but he was also clever. He looks at the woman indignantly and retorts: Go and see, the CCTV camera of my car is still working.

Story 34
Corruption

The Maharashtra government once advertise a tender about constructing a bridge. A manager is appointed in the office to take the quotation from private contractors. After reading the advertisement in newspapers, a lot of contractors flock to the office to have the deal. At first, a Tamilian contractor enters the office to submit the proposal. He says: It will cost three crore. The manager takes his quotation and instructs to wait outside.

After him, a Gujarati contractor submits the proposal. His quotation mentions - nine crore! The manager asks abruptly: Why so much? The cost is really very high! The Gujarati man replies: It is not high. In this, three crore is yours and three crore is mine. The manager enquires: Then who will construct the bridge? The man replies: The Tamilian guy will construct the bridge whom we'll pay the remaining three crore.

Story 35
Chain Marketing

A monkey lost his tail in childhood. All other monkeys of the forest taunt him by calling: Tail cut monkey. One day he makes a plan and tell other monkeys that as he doesn't have a tail, so he can see God. They all laugh at him but one says: Let me also see God. Now he says: For this, you have to get your tail cut. He agrees for losing his tail to God. As the first monkey cuts his tail, he cries: No, I can't see God. No, I can't see God.

The first one says: Shut up. I will cast a spell in your ear, then you can see God. Now he whispers into his ear: See, your tail is gone, if you say you can't see God, they'll also taunt you as they did to me. Better you say you see God. Now the second one shouts happily: Yes, I can see God. Yes, I can see God. And this way, all the monkeys lose their tails. This is what exactly happens in chain marketing business.

Story 36
Let Money Circulate

From this story, we will learn the importance of money being circulated. The circulation of money keeps the market up and moving. Let's start this story with an NRI who gets a newspaper one morning. He sees an advertisement of a beautiful hotel in int. Now he wants to book a room in the hotel, for which, he pays thousand rupees in advance and gets the room booked.

The hotel owner gives the same thousand rupee note to his vegetable wholesaler. The wholesaler, upon reaching home, gives the same note to a moneylender from whom he had taken a loan recently. Now the moneylender goes to the same hotel and books a room for himself. In the evening, the NRI cancels his booking. But the money already being circulated was moving things fast in market.

With your own addition and style, speak these stories in classroom without seeing notebooks. You can also speak with friends and do video-recording. Apply effective tone, emotion, correct pronunciation, good accent and diction.

Story 37
The Doctor's Skill

There was a doctor in a town. He puts a signboard stating: Get yourself cured from any disease for 500 rupees or take 1000 rupees back. A patient comes in and says: I have lost taste of my tongue. The doctor orders the nurse: Open 'Box 22' and give him four drops. The patient blurts out: It is petrol. The doctor responds fervently: You got your taste back, so pay 500 rupees. The patient goes out after paying, but he cultivates another plan. Next day again he comes complaining about another disease.

This time he reports having weak memory. The doctor orders the nurse again: Open 'Box 22' and…. The patient resists: But that is for taste. The doctor replies: You got your memory back, so pay 500 rupees. Next day again he comes complaining about weak eyesight. The doctor says: We have no cure for this, and you can take 1000 rupees. But while giving him money, he gives him only 500, on which, the patient reacts: It is 500. The doctor replies: You got your eyesight back, now pay 500 rupees.

Story 38
The Pathan's Promise

Let's talk about a Pathan who lived in Afghanistan a century ago. He had a very loving and gorgeous wife with whom he always kept promises. But one day his wife dies and he starts living restless. Many of his sympathizers condole him for his loss. But something strange starts happening. He regularly goes to the grave of his wife and moves hand-fan on it for hours. A passerby notices and remarks: What a great love!

Hesitatingly, the Pathan replies: It's not like that. My wife had asked me to remarry after the soil on her grave dried up. He enquires: Then what's the problem? Why don't you get married? The Pathan responds tenderly: But some rascal pours a bucket of water here every day. The passerby praises his fidelity for this wife but also advises him to catch the rascal and not waste time in moving the hand-fan.

With your own addition and style, speak these stories in classroom without seeing notebooks. You can also speak with friends and do video-recording. Apply effective tone, emotion, correct pronunciation, good accent and diction.

Story 39
The Secretary

This story starts with a business tycoon who lived in a city. One day he comes to a function with his secretary. But his wife, already present in function, stares at the secretary continually. So the secretary asks her boss: Why is your wife looking at me incessantly? The boss replies: Don't worry about her. Before marriage she was my secretary. And after the function ends, he sends her off and comes home with his wife.

By the time they reach home, it is late in night. When they go to bed, he notices that his wife's cellphone is ringing. He instructs her: If someone asks about me, tell that I am not at home. But the wife answers the call by saying: My husband is at home. The husband gets upset and enquires: Why did you say like that? Then she replies: The caller was my secretary, not yours. And the husband learns a big lesson!

Story 40
Lashkare Taliban

A businessman of Mumbai mistakenly puts balance in another phone number. He calls the number several times for refund, but his call is not received. He calls the customer care, but doesn't get solution from there too. Finally he plays a trick that works for his benefit. He sends a message: Welcome to Lashkare Taliban. You have become our member by accepting the balance. Now be careful while using your cellphone.

After sending the message, he starts waiting for the reply. In next five minutes, he gets a callback and the caller is really upset. He says: I don't want to become the member. The businessman asks: When I called you several times, why didn't you respond? The caller apologize for his mistake. Then the businessman replies: You must refund the money if you decline the membership. And this way, he gets the money back.

With your own addition and style, speak these stories in classroom without seeing notebooks. You can also speak with friends and do video-recording. Apply effective tone, emotion, correct pronunciation, good accent and diction.

Story 41
What is Advocacy?

In a class of law, an advocate was teaching advocacy to the students. He asks the students: Suppose two people come to me, one is clean and the other is dirty. I advise them to for a shower, now tell me who will bathe? The students say: The one who is dirty. The advocate says: No, the clean person will do because he has the habit of bathing. Now tell me who will bathe? The students say: The clean person. The advocate responds: No, the dirty person will bathe because he needs it. Now tell me who will bathe? The students say: The dirty person. The advocate adds further: No, both will bathe because the clean person has habit while the dirty one needs it. Now tell me who will bathe? The students say: Both. The advocate finally replies: Wrong, no one will bathe because dirty is not used to bathing and clean doesn't need to bathe.

Story 42
An Apple a Day

This is the story of a doctor and an engineer friends who lived in a city. They both were unmarried and looking for life partner. One day, they come to see a festival and get a chance to communicate with a female. Now both the doctor and the engineer fall in love with the same female friend. Feeling caring, they both come to give her a gift regularly. The doctor gives a rose daily but the engineer gives an apple daily.

The gift remains a secret between the two men. And one day, feeling confused about the apple, she decides to ask the reason from the engineer. When the engineer comes, she reveals: Your friend gives me a rose daily, which I find logical. There is a meaning of giving rose but why are you giving apple? Hearing this, the engineer smiles and replies: Because there is a saying - An apple a day keeps the doctor away.

With your own addition and style, speak these stories in classroom without seeing notebooks. You can also speak with friends and do video-recording. Apply effective tone, emotion, correct pronunciation, good accent and diction.

Story 43
Death of Jackal

There lived a husband and wife in Bangalore. The wife always claimed herself very intelligent, so the husband wanted to examine her. To check her intelligence, he asks if she gets lost in a forest, how would she come back home? The wife replies that she would look for a stone and then a jackal. But the husband cannot understand this logic so he asks her to explain.

She adds further that she would hit the jackal with the stone and run behind him. The husband curiously asks how he would bring her home. Now she elaborates: Because people say – When the jackal is to die, he runs towards the city. So she wants to prove that by following him, she will come out of the forest. The husband understands her level of intelligence and doesn't want to enquire anything further.

Story 44
Men Will Be Men

This is the story of a warrior king who lived in a territory. Facing some challenges, he plans a warfare against his opponent. Considering it a lethal battle, he locks the room of his dearest and beautiful wife and gives the key to his special friend. He says: If I don't return in four days, you can open the lock and she will be yours. After saying this, he marches ahead on a horse for the war. He keeps moving in the desert.

After an hour, the king sees someone coming behind with dust and noises. He stops and gets ready to fight. When closely noticing, he finds that it was his same friend coming fast on a horse who was given the key. The king enquires: What happened? The friend takes a long breath and replies: The key you gave me is wrong! Obviously, men will be men.

With your own addition and style, speak these stories in classroom without seeing notebooks. You can also speak with friends and do video-recording. Apply effective tone, emotion, correct pronunciation, good accent and diction.

Story 45
Liquor in Boat

This is the story of a voyage in Europe. Once there was a captain and an assistant in a boat. They were sailing for an African country and it was a long journey to complete. Spending several days and nights, the assistant drinks liquor one day. The captain, who hated liquor the most, notices him drinking. And while writing a diary for the supervisor, the captain mentions that — Today the assistant drank liquor.

The assistant reads, but unable to do anything, he keeps silence and waits for his time. The next day, it was the assistant's turn to write the diary. So he writes in night — Today the captain did not drink liquor. When the captain reads, he gets shocked seeing the sentence giving a different meaning. Sensing it dangerous for his job, he apologizes to the assistant and decides to throw the diary in water.

Story 46
Acid Effect

A chemical factory in Chennai had recently recruited some new staffs. The management decided to get them trained so there were called in a science lab for training. All the new employees, sitting as audience had to learn about the effect of acid. The chemist comes on the stage with a glass filled with acid. Then he takes a coin from his pocket and drops into the glass. And then he asks the employees: Tell me, will this coin get dissolved in acid?

He waits a few seconds and sees a hand lifting up. One of the employees stands up to respond. He replies: No sir, it won't dissolve. The chemist nodes his head and chuckles at him. Then he enquires: Very good, but how did you know that? The employee responds: Sir, if acid would dissolve a coin, you would have taken my coin, not yours. And the chemist realizes that the employee is absolutely right.

Story 47
Chocolate Tricks

The two boys named Jillson and Billson were talking to each other. They were in front of a chocolate shop. Jillson says: I'm so clever that I can steal chocolates and the shopkeeper won't notice. Now Billson says: I'm so clever that that he will give me chocolates for free. Jillson laughs and challenges Billson. They enter the shop and Jillson succeeds in stealing two chocolate without letting the shopkeeper notice. Now he asks Billson to play his trick.

Billson opens the chocolate jar, takes all eight chocolates out and puts them back in. The shopkeeper notices and realizes something fishy. He tells that there were ten chocolates in the jar. Billson responds: We're are here, you can search where the chocolates are. The shopkeeper takes out the chocolates from Jillson's pocket, and gives one to Billson as a reward.

Story 48
Let the Game Get Going

A young boy enters a salon and the barber whispers to his customer: This is the dumbest kid in the world. Watch while I prove it to you. The barber puts a dollar bill in one hand and two quarters in the other, then he calls the boy over and asks: Which do you we want, son? The boy takes the quarters and leaves. The customer sees that the barber was right.

Later, when the customer leaves the salon, he sees the same young boy coming out of the ice cream store. He says: Hey, son! May I ask you a question? Why did you take the quarters instead of the dollar bill? The boy licks his cone and replies: Because the day I take the dollar, the game is over! So, let the game get going.

With your own addition and style, speak these stories in classroom without seeing notebooks. You can also speak with friends and do video-recording. Apply effective tone, emotion, correct pronunciation, good accent and diction.

Story 49
The Sweet Shop

Sweets are famous in West Bengal and this is the story of a sweet shop located in Kolkata. An uncle visited this shop every day and he used to see a small girl sitting at the counter. Out of curiously, he wanted to ask couple of questions to the girl. He enquires: Are you able to run this shop properly? The girl confidently responds: Yes uncle. Now the uncle looks at the shop full of various kinds of sweets.

He adds the next question: Don't you feel urge of eating these sweets when you are alone? The girl replies: I feel a lot. But there is a problem. If one sweet falls short, my father will scold me a lot. He feels there is some secret that she wants to reveal. "Then what you do?" asks the uncle. The girl finally responds: So I lick all of them and put back in.

Story 50
Manipulation

This is the story of a father and son who lived in America. The father was considered a great visionary in the society. One day, the father tells his son that he wants him to marry a girl of his choice. The son denies his request. Then the father says that the girl is the daughter of Bill Gates. Now the son promptly agrees. In his next plan, he goes to Bill Gates and says: I want your daughter to marry my son. But Bill Gates denies.

The father tells Bill Gates that his son is the CEO of the World Bank. Hearing about the World Bank, Bill Gates agrees for marriage. Now the father goes to the President of the World Bank and tells him to appoint his son as the CEO of his bank. When the President denies, he says that his son is the son-in-law of Bill Gates. And the President confirms his son's appointment. Sometimes, manipulation is something that works!

With your own addition and style, speak these stories in classroom without seeing notebooks. You can also speak with friends and do video-recording. Apply effective tone, emotion, correct pronunciation, good accent and diction.

FreeFlow Speaking

Unlimited speaking subjects on informative facts.
This is good for knowledge enhancement.
You can make short changes if required.
In speaking in classroom, apply energy and enthusiasm.
Use correct pronunciation and good accent and diction.

FreeFlow 1
Dell Corporation

Dell Corporation was established in 1984 in the USA.
The founder of this company is Michael Dell.
He was born in 1965 in the state of Texas.
He worked first at a Chinese restaurant to earn money.
Then he started the business of upgrading computers.
In 1984 Michael registered his company as PC's Limited.
Same year, he changed it to Dell Corporation.
Dell ranked top 500 companies of the world.
It started earning great by selling computers on web.
He has worked as an advisor of the US President's Council.
He resides at Austin in Texas with wife and three children.
Dell's net worth is estimated $ 15 billion.

FreeFlow 2
Apple Foundation

Apple was established in a garage of San Francisco in 1976.
Its founder Steve Jobs was born in 1955 in the USA.
His father was a machinist and mother was a clerk.
Steve got educated up to intermediate.
He attended HP computer lectures at Palo Alto, California.
Later Steve was hired there on temporary basis.
He dropped out college because of money problem.
He got a technician job for Atari company,
He travelled India to know about Buddhism.
He established Apple company in his parents' garage.
Apple invented Macintosh computer operating system.
Apple's products are iPod, iTunes, and iPhones.
It has the highest brand value in the entire world.

These are unlimited speaking topics based on interesting facts. You speak these topics in classroom limitlessly using correct accent and diction with energy and enthusiasm. These topics are also good for knowledge improvement.

FreeFlow 3
Facebook

The founder of Facebook is Mark Zuckerberg.
It was launched in 2004 from Cambridge, Massachusetts.
After launching, Mark was charged with breach of Cambridge's security.
To prepare this website, Mark hacked into his college's network.
Its first name was Facemash which became Facebook in 2005.
Facebook was initially used for sharing college notes and photos.
In 2004, Sean Parker became the president of Facebook.
It established its headquarter at Palo Alto, California.
They received first investment from Pay Pal company.
They earn most of revenue from advertisement.
Microsoft is the exclusive partner of Facebook.

FreeFlow 4
Hollywood

Hollywood is an area in Los Angeles, California.
It is the hub of many world famous film studios.
Columbia Pictures, Disney, and Warner Bros are also here.
Hollywood was incorporated as a municipality in 1903.
It was consolidated with Los Angeles city.
After consolidation, film industry emerged here.
It was developed by builder and constructor Whitley.
America had first film industry in Jacksonville, Florida.
Hollywood giving warm winter attracted film companies.
Kalem Studios was the first to arrive in 1908.
Hollywood influences culture and economy of the world.
Avatar is the most successful Hollywood movie.

These are unlimited speaking topics based on interesting facts. You speak these topics in classroom limitlessly using correct accent and diction with energy and enthusiasm. These topics are also good for knowledge improvement.

FreeFlow 5
Mummy

A mummy is a dead human or animal.
The word mummy is taken from Arabic: mumiya.
Mumiya means 'tar' in Arabic and Persian language.
Mummification is to embalming a dead to keep indestructible.
The body was embalmed, wrapped and kept in a coffin.
It started in Egypt around 2600 BC.
This activity faded after Rome started ruling over Egypt.
It was stopped at the arrival of Christianity.
The purpose was to keep the body intact for heavenly use.
The believed in the possibility of life after death.

FreeFlow 6
Vatican City

Vatican City is the home of pope and roman bureaus.
It is the smallest nation in the world.
It is total population of 825 people.
Vatican has the area of 110 acres surrounded by Rome.
It became independent from Italy in 1929.
The independence treaty was between King Victor 8th and Pope.
It enables the pope to exercise his universal authority.
This independence treaty was authorized by Mussolini.
Vatican came twice under small attacks in World War 2.
It has most famous religious and cultural sites.
Vatican City uses Italian and Latin language.

These are unlimited speaking topics based on interesting facts. You speak these topics in classroom limitlessly using correct accent and diction with energy and enthusiasm. These topics are also good for knowledge improvement.

FreeFlow 7
William Shakespeare

Shakespeare was born in 1564 in Stratford, England.
He was the son of John and Mary Shakespeare.
He had eight siblings and he was the eldest of them.
William's father was prosecuted for black marketing in wool gathering.
William attended King Edward School from the age of seven.
When he was eighteen, he married twenty-six years old Anne Hathaway.
They had three children, but after marriage, William left for London.
He started working for a playing company giving food to horses.
Later he developed the skill of playwriting.
In 1594, he Shakespeare became the part-owner of a playing company.
Later his company was adopted by a king for support.
After two years, William also became an actor.
He died in 1616 at the age of 52 at Strafford.
His famous plays are Hamlet, Julius Caesar, The Tempest, Romeo and Juliet.

FreeFlow 8
Rowan Atkinson

Rowan Atkinson is known as the world famous comedian Mr. Bean.
He was born in 1955 at Durham, England, United Kingdom.
His father Eric was a farming company director.
He graduated from Queen's College, Oxford in Electrical Engineering.
Rowan initially acted for Oxford University dramatic society.
He was first starred in a BBC comedy show named 'Atkinson People'.
Atkinson also worked for James Bond movie Never Say Never Again.
Mr. Bean, a half hour comedy show first appeared on TV in 1990.
He also worked for Just For Laughs, and then got two movies.
Rowan became a super comedian from the movie Johnny English.
His other famous movies are Rat Race, Love Actually, Ultimate Disaster.
Rowan married Sunetra Sastry who was working as a BBC makeup artist.
He was formerly in relationship with actress Leslie Ash.

These are unlimited speaking topics based on interesting facts. You speak these topics in classroom limitlessly using correct accent and diction with energy and enthusiasm. These topics are also good for knowledge improvement.

FreeFlow 9
Reliance

Dhirubhai Ambani is the founder of Reliance.
He founded this company in 1954 in Ahmadabad, Gujarat.
He was born in 1932 in a low income family of Chorwad, Gujarat.
His father Hirachand was a school teacher at Chorwad.
Dhirubhai's first work was to sell potato fries on weekends.
He went to Aden (Greece) to work after matriculation.
He learnt English grammar and essay writing.
Dhirubhai opened the first textile mill Ahmadabad in 1954.
He started selling polyester cloth from Masjid Bunder, Mumbai.
Reliance established its first plant in 1982 competing Bombay Dying.
He also had enmity with Indian Express newspaper.
Dhirubhai Ambani is considered the great wealth creator.

FreeFlow 10
Google

Google was founded by Larry Page and Sergey Brin.
It was established in 1998 in California, USA.
Google works for Internet, Cloud computing, Artificial intelligence.
Google has one lakh thirty-five thousand employees worldwide.
It is a global establishment with offices in fifty countries.
Its popular products are Gmail, YouTube, Google Translate.
Google leads in mobile operating system.
Almost 71 percent people use Google Android cellphones.
Google Chrome is the best and simple web browser.
Google.com is the most visited website worldwide.
Its current CEO is Sundar Pichai, and CFO is Ruth Porat.

These are unlimited speaking topics based on interesting facts. You speak these topics in classroom limitlessly using correct accent and diction with energy and enthusiasm. These topics are also good for knowledge improvement.

FreeFlow 11
Niagara Falls

Niagara Falls is a group of three waterfalls.
It is located at the border of the US and Canada.
It is formed by the Niagara River of Lake Erie.
This place was named after Niagagarega tribe.
It is also considered the world's fastest moving waterfall.
The fall is 188 feet tall and 170 feet deep.
It started forming around twelve thousand years ago.
It happened with the effect of glacier activity.
Niagara Falls also produces large amount of electricity.
The beauty of this site attract many visitors globally.
It provides 20% of drinking water to the USA.
Vising this place is really joyful in summer season.

FreeFlow 12
Great Wall of China

The Great Wall of China is a series of protection wall.
The construction was started in 3rd century BC by King Qin Shi Huang.
The purpose was to protect China from barbarous nomadic people.
It is a series of 19 walls in 21 thousand kilometers.
It took 20 years in constructing each wall and 9 dynasties worked for it.
The Great Wall is between north China and south Mongolia.
The wall is 16 to 26 feet high and 1.5 feet thick.
Badaling is a place for most visitors to view the Great Wall.
Badaling is eighty kilometers far from Beijing.
It is considered a masterpiece on the earth.
This wall is also the symbol of Chinese identity and culture.
The Great Wall is one of the seven old wonders of the world.

These are unlimited speaking topics based on interesting facts. You speak these topics in classroom limitlessly using correct accent and diction with energy and enthusiasm. These topics are also good for knowledge improvement.

FreeFlow 13
Geoffrey Chaucer

Geoffrey Chaucer is regarded as the father of English literature.
He was born in 1343 in a business class family of London.
His father and grandfather were the wine merchants in London.
His family name 'chaucer' derives from French meaning 'shoemaker'.
Geoffrey studied law and joined the royal court of King Edward 3rd.
He also learnt Latin, French and Italian languages.
Geoffrey also maintained an active career in civil service.
He achieved fame as author, philosopher, and astronomer.
He is a crucial figure in developing English from French and Latin.
Chaucer is widely considered the greatest English poet.
He is best known for the anthology named the Canterbury Tales.
Geoffrey Chaucer died in October 1400 in London.

FreeFlow 14
Cleopatra

Cleopatra was a queen and last active ruler of Egypt.
She is famous for relations with highest number of men in the world.
Cleopatra was born in Alexandria, Egypt in 69 BC.
Her father Ptolemy 8th was the king of Egypt.
She was in relationship with Roman statesman Julius Caesar.
Cleopatra came to power with the support of Julius Caesar.
She ruled over Egypt in the last century of BC up to 21 years.
She was the descendant of the companion of Alexander Great.
Her native language was Greek but she learnt Egyptian.
She actively influenced Roman politics at a crucial period.
Her life inspired numerous books, plays, and movies.
She ended her life at the age of 39 when her husband Anthony died.
She is considered one of the beautiful women of the world.

These are unlimited speaking topics based on interesting facts. You speak these topics in classroom limitlessly using correct accent and diction with energy and enthusiasm. These topics are also good for knowledge improvement.

FreeFlow 15
ICICI Bank

ICICI stands for Industrial Credit & Investment Corporation of India.
It is an Indian multinational bank and financial services company.
It was founded in 1994 in Vadodara, Gujarat.
This bank has six thousand offices all over India.
ICICI is being operated worldwide from the year of 1999.
It has branches also in UK, US, Canada, Russia, and Singapore.
The chairman of this establishment is Girish Chandra Chaturvedi.
The CEO and managing director's name is Sandeep Bakshi.
ICICI is mainly in retail banking, investment, and mortgage.
It has eighty-five thousand employees in India.
This bank launched Internet Banking operation in 1998.
ICICI Bank is one of the Big Four banks of India.

FreeFlow 16
McDonald's

McDonald's is an American fast food company.
It was founded in 1940 as a restaurant in California.
This company was founded by Richard and Maurice McDonald.
McDonald's had first started selling hamburger in California.
This establishment sold it first franchise in 1955.
McDonald's is the world's largest restaurant chain.
It has 38 thousand outlets in one hundred countries.
It servers seventy million customers daily in the world.
This eatery is best known for hamburger, French fries, soft drink.
McDonald's has the ninth highest global brand value.
McDonald's franchise fee is Rs. 30 lakh in India.
In India, McDonald's has the largest outlet in Guwahati, Assam.

These are unlimited speaking topics based on interesting facts. You speak these topics in classroom limitlessly using correct accent and diction with energy and enthusiasm. These topics are also good for knowledge improvement.

FreeFlow 17
Microsoft Windows

Windows is a graphical operating system.
It is developed and marketed globally by Microsoft.
Microsoft was founded by Bill Gates and Paul Allen.
Windows was first released in 1985 as Windows 1.
This operating system is available in 110 different languages.
Before Windows, people used to work computer using MS-DOS.
This operating system spread over 90% of computer market.
It had competition with Mac operating system of Apple.
Windows' initial name was Interface Manager.
Windows XP was the best version of Windows operating system.
Microsoft has released the latest version as Windows 365.
Satya Nadella is the current CEO of Microsoft.

FreeFlow 18
YouTube

YouTube is an American online video platform.
It has headquarter in San Bruno, California, USA.
YouTube was launched in 2005 by Steve Chen and Jawed Karim.
YouTube is owned by Google and it is the second popular site.
Google bought YouTube after ten months of its launch.
The first most visited website is Google Search.
YouTube has more than 2.5 billion monthly users.
The users watch more than one billion hours video daily.
This platform earns from advertisement while watching videos.
YouTube's monthly revenue is around one billion dollars.
It was created in most popular Python programming language.
YouTube has more than eighty million premium users.

FreeFlow 19
Sunny Leone

Sunny Leone's real name is Karenjit Kaur Vohra.
She was born in 1981 in a Sikh family in Ontario, Canada.
As a first work, Sunny Leone worked for a German bakery.
Later she worked as an assistant for a tax and retirement firm.
She started modelling as her hobby and posed for Penthouse magazine.
Later she appeared for other magazines such as High Society, Swank.
From 2005, she started working for Vivid Entertainment in intimate movies.
Next year, Sunny also became an American citizen.
Same year, she first appeared in a music award on MTV India.
Later she participated in Bigg Boss reality show.
Sunny Leone married her fellow actor Daniel Weber.
At present, she is the hot choice of film producers in India.

FreeFlow 20
Charlie Chaplin

Charlie Chaplin was a famous comedian of the world.
He was born in 1889 in London, England.
Charlie's parents were music hall entertainers in London.
Charlie spent childhood in poverty at Walworth, South London.
He was sent to work at the age of seven, but later joined a school.
When he was nine, his mother fell into mental disorder.
Through father's contact, Charlie joined a dancing group.
At the age of thirteen, he abandoned education and became an actor.
Within five years, Chaplin became a famous comedy performer.
He was invited to join New York Motion Pictures Company.
Charlie rose to fame by performing in several movies of silent era.
He married four times and had eleven children.
Charlie Chaplin died in 1977 in Switzerland.

These are unlimited speaking topics based on interesting facts. You speak these topics in classroom limitlessly using correct accent and diction with energy and enthusiasm. These topics are also good for knowledge improvement.

FreeFlow 21
Adolf Hitler

Adolf Hitler was born in 1889 at Linz, Austria.
He moved to Germany at the age of 24 and joined army.
He fought as a German soldier in World War First.
Later he joined and became the leader of German Workers' Party.
After two years, he staged a power conspiracy in Munich.
This conspiracy caused him one year imprisonment.
His autobiography and charismatic oratory made him famous.
Adolf Hitler merged with Nazi Party and won the election.
This way he became the dictator chancellor of Germany.
He stood to fight against Jews, Britain, and France.
His aggressiveness caused fast economic recovery but started World War 2.
During World War 2, German forces occupied most of Europe and north Africa.
Adolf married his long time beloved Eva Braun in 1945.
His unsuccessful attempt to win over Russia made him to end his life.

FreeFlow 22
Galileo Galilei

Galileo Galilei was born in 1564 in Pisa, Italy.
He is regarded as the father of physics.
In his childhood, his family moved to Florence for better lifestyle.
He studied mathematics and astronomy and became a math's professor.
He is also known as a mathematician, astronomer and philosopher.
Without marriage, with Marina, he had two daughters and one son.
His achievement includes the improvement to the telescope.
On his statement: The sun is the center of universe, he faced criticism.
He also said: The scripture is a book of poetry and songs, not instructions.
Later the Catholic Church condemned his views publically.
The church arrested him and ordered in-house captivity for lifetime.
During his 70's, he went blind a developed lots of physical complications.
Recently the pope accepted the mistake committed by the church.
The Vatican proposed erect a statue of him inside the walls.
He died in 1642 in Florence at the age of 77.

These are unlimited speaking topics based on interesting facts. You speak these topics in classroom limitlessly using correct accent and diction with energy and enthusiasm. These topics are also good for knowledge improvement.

FreeFlow 23
Netflix

Netflix is an over-the-top video platform.
It also works as a film production company.
Netflix has headquarter in Los Gatos, California, USA.
It was founded in 1997 by Reed Hastings and Marc Randolph.
In 2021, Netflix had 209 million subscribers worldwide.
This company's starting business was selling and renting DVDs.
Netflix introduced streaming media in 2007 much before Amazon.
This company also entered in content production with their associates.
Its first video show is – House of Cards.
Netflix released 126 series and films in 2016.
In 2020, Netflix became the largest entertainment company.
The show 'Red Notice' is the most successful Netflix movie.

FreeFlow 24
Oxford

Oxford is a renowned university in England.
It was founded in 9th century by King Alfred the Great.
It got well-constructed and started teaching from 1096.
Oxford is made up of 39 colleges in Oxford city of England.
This university operates the world's oldest university museum.
It has the largest university press in the world.
This university has educated 28 prime ministers of the UK.
Seventy-two Nobel Prize laureates also come from this university.
Its alumni have won 160 Olympic medals.
It grew in 11th century when England's students returned from Paris.
This university is famous for research, teaching and innovation.
Indian students are counted as the fifth largest for Oxford.

These are unlimited speaking topics based on interesting facts. You speak these topics in classroom limitlessly using correct accent and diction with energy and enthusiasm. These topics are also good for knowledge improvement.

FreeFlow 25
Charles Babbage

Charles Babbage is regarded as the father of computer.
He was born in 1791 at Walworth Road, London.
His father Benjamin Babbage was a banking partner.
Charles couldn't attend schools because of his mental illness.
His parents arranged tutors for his education.
He studied mathematics deeply and became a professor in Cambridge.
Babbage won gold medal for teaching at Cambridge University.
His father, wife and son, all died in 1827.
These deaths caused him to go into mental breakdown.
Charles sought a method of calculating tables without human errors.
Babbage invented the machine in 1822 and named Analytical Engine.
Charles Babbage died in 1871 at Marylebone, London.
His half brain is kept at Hunterian Museum in Royal College.
And the other half is in Science Museum of London.

FreeFlow 26
Homi Jehangir Bhabha

Bhabha is regarded as the father of Indian nuclear program.
He was also the founding director of Atomic Energy Establishment.
This establishment is now known as Bhabha Atomic Research Center.
Homi Jehangir was awarded the Adams Prize and Padma Bhushan.
He was also nominated for the Nobel Prize for physics.
Homi was born in 1909 in a Parsi family in Mumbai.
His father Hormusji Bhabha was an aristocratic lawyer.
Homi studied as Elphinstone College and joined Cambridge.
He did PhD in theoretical physics while working in a laboratory.
His development in atomic energy made him internationally famous.
He served as the president of the U.N's Atomic Conference.
He died in 1966 in an airplane crash in France.

These are unlimited speaking topics based on interesting facts. You speak these topics in classroom limitlessly using correct accent and diction with energy and enthusiasm. These topics are also good for knowledge improvement.

FreeFlow 27
Leonardo da Vinci

Leonardo da Vinci is considered the greatest painter of the world.
Leonardo was born in 1452 in Vinci, Florence, Italy.
He was an illegitimate son of Piero and Caterina.
He was educated in the studio of Florence by painter Verrocchio.
Leonardo became famous as a painter for the painting of Monalisa.
He received an informal education of Latin, geometry and mathematics.
His painting of 'Baptism of Christ' became superior to his master's.
In second Italian war, he was employed as a military engineer.
He spent last years of life living in the Vatican City.
In his last days, he called a priest and got baptized to Christianity.
He had no close relationship with women and kept his life secret.
Leonardo da Vinci was once prosecuted for homosexuality.
Da Vinci died in 1519 at Clos Luce in France.

FreeFlow 28
Christopher Columbus

Christopher Columbus is regarded as the discoverer of America.
He was born in 1451 in the city of Genoa, Italy (then Spain).
He spent childhood working at his family's cheese shop.
Then he worked on a ship to support the king in warfare.
Christopher married Filipa who was Portugal governor's daughter.
From 1482, he started trading along the coasts of West Africa.
After his wife's death, he found a mistress in Spain to live with.
He studied Latin, Portuguese, astronomy, geography, history and Bibile
Columbus estimated westward route shorter for Asia for spice trading.
Spanish queen Isabella supported his voyage and exploration.
His proposal was a matter of disbelief as it was impossible to return alive.
Columbus departed from Spain with 3 ships for 5 weeks' of voyage.
Assuming East Asia, he reached Bahamas' island which he named San Salvador.
Columbus mistook it for India and referred to the inhabitants as Indians.
After seven months he returned to Spain with 9 natives alive.
At death in 1506 also he was convinced that he had voyaged to Asia.

FreeFlow 29
White House

White House is the residence and workplace of US president.
White House is located at Pennsylvania in Washington DC.
It was designed by architect of Washington named James Hoban.
The construction of this house started in 1792.
The total cost of constructing this house was 2.5 lakh dollars.
It was first occupied by President John Adams in 1800.
In 1814, this house was partly burnt by British Army.
This residence is made up of six stories with 132 rooms.
It is also a symbol which represents American democracy.
White House comes under heritage of National Park Service.
Its old name till 18th century was the President's Palace.
In 1901, President Roosevelt named it The White House.
We can see White House from Pennsylvania Avenue.

FreeFlow 30
Amazon

Amazon is an American e-commerce company.
The founder of this company is Jeff Bezos.
It is one of the Big Five info-tech business firm worldwide.
It focuses on e-commerce, cloud computing, and streaming.
Amazon was launched in 1994 with name Cadabra.
It started with the first work as selling books online.
Now Amazon Prime facilitates video shows.
This company has headquarter in Seattle, Washington.
In 2021, it was the world's largest online retailer.
Amazon Prime has 200 million online subscribers.
It is the second largest company in America after Walmart.
Amazon is the most customer centric organization.

These are unlimited speaking topics based on interesting facts. You speak these topics in classroom limitlessly using correct accent and diction with energy and enthusiasm. These topics are also good for knowledge improvement.

FreeFlow 31
Coca-Cola

Coca-Cola or Coke is a soft drink by Coca-Cola Company.
It was invented as a non-alcoholic drink in nineteenth century.
John Pemberton of Atlanta, Georgia invented this drink.
Coca means 'coca leaves' and cola means 'kola nuts'.
There two ingredients are also used in caffeine.
Caffeine is a psychoactive stimulant available in coffee.
The current formula of Coca-Cola is a close secret.
It is the world's sixth most valuable brand.
This soft drink is sold in two hundred countries worldwide.
Coca-Cola also received Best Bottling Company award.
Its logo was designed by Frank Robinson in 1885.
Coca-Cola is a global symbol of American tastes.
Coke doesn't sell only drink but also happiness.

FreeFlow 32
Wikipedia

Wikipedia is a free online encyclopedia.
It is maintained by its community of volunteers.
Wikipedia is the largest and most-read online page.
It is one of the fifteen most popular websites.
This site is hosted by American non-profit organization.
This organization is mainly funded by donations.
Wikipedia was launched by Jimmy Wales and Larry Sanger.
This online portal started in 2001 in San Francisco, USA.
It is available in 327 languages with no advertisement.
Wikipedia was earlier known as Nupedia.
In 2007, this website got 43 million unique visitors.
Wikipedia English has more than 42 million registered users.
India is second after USA in using Wikipedia.

These are unlimited speaking topics based on interesting facts. You speak these topics in classroom limitlessly using correct accent and diction with energy and enthusiasm. These topics are also good for knowledge improvement.

FreeFlow 33
Sudha Chandran

Sudha Chandran is a Bharatanatyam dancer and actress.
She was born in 1965 in a Tamil family in Mumbai.
Her father K.D Chandran was an actor in Mumbai.
When she was eighteen, she lost her right leg in an accident.
Sudha however continued dancing and got established.
She is known for her role of Ramola Sikand in Kahin Kisi Roz.
Chandran did M.A in economics from Mithibai College, Mumbai.
She started acting for Telugu film Mayuri based on her life.
The film was remade in Hindi as Naache Mayuri.
Sudha got two awards for her role in Mayuri.
She is given an honorary doctorate degree by Bareily University.
Sudha Chandran married assistant director Ravi Dang.
Her biography is a part of education for school children.

FreeFlow 34
Michael Jackson

Michael Jackson is regarded as the best pop music entertainer of all time.
He is was a singer, dancer, musician and also lyricist and philanthropist.
He was born in 1958 in an Afro-American labor family of Indiana.
He had 10 siblings and he received extreme stress of poverty.
His father used to beat and abuse him of having a fat nose.
At the age of 6, he joined a small music band as a backup musician.
He grew up performing backup vocals and dancing.
At the age of 8, he began lead vocals in striptease adult dance.
In 1980, he became the king of pop music, rock, funk, jack swing, and disco.
He had multiple Grammy Awards, American Music Awards, and World Records,
He married twice and was supporting 39 charities
Up to 45 years, he remained a dominant figure in music sensation.
He was invited to the White House to receive award from President Reagan.
In house, he had Ferris wheel, theatre, and 40 patrolling guards.
He died in 2009 in his bed at Los Angeles.

These are unlimited speaking topics based on interesting facts. You speak these topics in classroom limitlessly using correct accent and diction with energy and enthusiasm. These topics are also good for knowledge improvement.

FreeFlow 35
Bruce Lee

Bruce Lee is regarded as the most prominent martial artist of all time.
He was a Hong Kong and American popular figure.
He was also an actor, director, producer, and philosopher.
He was considered a pop culture icon of 20th century.
Bruce Lee bridged the gap between East World and West World.
He changed the way Asians were presented in American films.
Lee was born in 1940 in San Francisco, America.
Lee had the citizenship of the US and Hong Kong.
His parents performed as opera actors in Hong Kong.
He acted as a child artist and later learnt and performed martial art.
He took admission in Washington University and also continued martial art.
Bruce Lee won six awards as a martial artist actor.
In 1973, Bruce Lee collapsed to death in a film studio.

FreeFlow 36
Marvan Atapattu

Marvan Atapattu is the rarest and prolific batsman of Sri Lanka.
He has scored five thousand runs in Test matches.
His career is considered crucial in the world of cricket.
Marvan was born in 1970 in Kalutara, Sri Lanka.
At the age of twenty, he entered international cricket.
But in his initial six years, he could score only 1 run.
He was insulted and dismissed two times form his team.
Marvan was considered not-made for international cricket.
But his good score in domestic matches got him a chance again.
For the next 11 innings, he could not score above 29 runs.
But in his tenth match against India, he hit first century.
He registered highest Test score of 249 runs against Zimbabwe.
Atapattu is also a skillful fielder with an accurate throw.
Marvan Atapattu has made 16 centuries and 6 double centuries.

These are unlimited speaking topics based on interesting facts. You speak these topics in classroom limitlessly using correct accent and diction with energy and enthusiasm. These topics are also good for knowledge improvement.

FreeFlow 37
Opera House

The Opera House in Sydney is the performing art center.
It is located on the banks of beautiful Sydney Harbor.
This house is regarded as the masterpiece of 20ᵗʰ century.
It was designed by Australian architect Jorn Utzon.
The magnificent construction was completed by Peter Hall in 1973.
The final cost was 102 million dollars and was paid by a State Lottery.
Opera House is the best known landmark of the capital of Australia.
It has 2679-seat concert hall to enjoy multiple performing arts.
It hosts to symphony concerts, choir performances, and music shows.
This house was inaugurated by Queen Elizabeth 2ⁿᵈ.
Its gleaming beauty attracts visitors from all over the world.
The Opera House is the most photographed building globally.
More than 11 million people visit the Opera House every year.

FreeFlow 38
Adidas

Adidas is a German clothes and shoes company.
It has headquarter located in the city of Bavaria, Germany.
Adidas was started in 1924 by the businessman Adolf Dassler.
He named it by merging his first and last name.
Adidas is the second largest sportswear manufacturer.
Adolf had started this company in his mother's house.
He got the idea of this business after returning from World War 1.
He was joined by his elder brother Rudolf Dassler.
Adolf first developed spiked running shoes.
His brother later separated and established Puma company.
Puma and Nike companies are the rivals of Adidas.
The first American runner Jesse wore Adidas shoes in Olympics.
Adidas was selling 200 thousand pair of shoes in World War 2.

These are unlimited speaking topics based on interesting facts. You speak these topics in classroom limitlessly using correct accent and diction with energy and enthusiasm. These topics are also good for knowledge improvement.

FreeFlow 39
José Salvador (hozey)

José Salvador Alvarenga is the longest solo survivor at sea.
His story of bravery is the most surprising in the world.
Alvarenga was born in 1975 in the country of El Salvador, near Mexico.
He was an experienced sailor and fisherman fishing in deep-sea.
In November 2012, he departed from a village of Mexico with a mate.
José hoped to catch sharks, marlins, and sailfish.
Shortly after embarking, his small boat was blown off by a storm.
During this, the motor and most of essential things of him got damaged.
Alvarenga called his boss on a radio for help but the battery died soon.
Having no support system, the boat began to wander in the open sea.
The search organized by Alvarenga's employer failed to find his trace.
They survived upon frogs, birds, ice, and rain water.
But in the third month, his mate died because of starvation.
After 438 days, in January 2014, Alvarenga was found near Australia.

FreeFlow 40
Nando Parrado

Nando Parrado is one of the 16 Uruguay plane crash survivors.
His story of bravery with his friend Roberto Canessa is the rarest.
A rugby team of Uruguay was scheduled to play against the team of Chile.
The Uruguay team got into an airplane to go through Andes mountain.
The mountain is 17,000 feet tall and 9,000 km long.
Sadly, the plane with 45 people crashed in the mountain in Argentina.
It took life 12 people and 33 remained alive at the peak of Andes.
Several rescue operations by 3 countries but none could find them.
In 62 days of dreadful struggle to survive, 17 died in starvation.
Still no way to live, Nando and Roberto decided to come down.
They had to walk up to 50 miles to see some humans in Chile.
Then the entire team was rescued after 72 days of crash.
This plane crash is portrayed in the 1993 feature film Alive.

These are unlimited speaking topics based on interesting facts. You speak these topics in classroom limitlessly using correct accent and diction with energy and enthusiasm. These topics are also good for knowledge improvement.

FreeFlow 41
Mirza Ghalib

Mirza Ghalib is the popular poet of Urdu and Persian language.
His full name is Mirza Asadullah Baig Khan.
His fame is seen in all three countries of Indian diaspora.
He is considered the last great poet of the Mughal Era.
Ghalib was born in 1797 at Kala Mahal, Agra, India.
At the age of thirteen, Ghalib married Umrao Begum.
After marriage, he settled in Ballimaran, Chandni Chowk, Delhi.
None of his seven children survived beyond infancy.
He served as an important courtier of king Bahadur Shah 2nd.
Ghalib was also appointed as a poetry tutor of the emperor.
His poetries encompass love, loss, betrayal, and Sufi mysticism.
He died in 1869 at his mansion in Chandni Chowk.
His house has been turned into Ghalib Memorial and Exhibition.
Ghalib's fame came after his death from the next generation.

FreeFlow 42
Jamshedji Tata

Jamshedji Tata is regarded as the father of Indian Industry.
He was an Indian pioneer industrialist who founded Tata Group.
He was born in 1839 in a Parsi family at Navsari, Vadodara, Gujarat.
His father had an established export trading firm in Mumbai.
He joined his father's work and also enrolled at Elphinstone College.
Tata married Hirabai and they had two sons.
Jamshedji founded his own trading company in 1868.
His business expanded in in steel, education, hotel, and electricity.
Tata steel is Asia's first and India's largest company.
Jamshedji also established Jamshedpur city in Jharkhand.
Indian Institute of Science in Bengaluru is established by Tata group.
Jamshedji Tata died in 1904 at the age of 65 in Germany.

These are unlimited speaking topics based on interesting facts. You speak these topics in classroom limitlessly using correct accent and diction with energy and enthusiasm. These topics are also good for knowledge improvement.

FreeFlow 43
Great Pyramid of Giza

It is one of the oldest seven wonders of ancient world.
This pyramid is a tomb of Egyptian king pharaoh.
This pyramid was built in 26th century BC in Egypt.
Giza is the second largest city in Egypt after Cairo.
This is the tallest man-made structure of ancient time.
This pyramid can be seen with the altitude of 481 feet.
It has the grave of Pharaoh Khufu who had died in 2.600 BC.
Therefore this pyramid is roughly 4,500 years old.
This monument is the relic of Egypt's old kingdom.
This structure was designed by Khufu's relative Hemiunu.
This pyramid got global fame in the 17th century CE.
It is a reminder of ancient Egyptian glorification of life after death

FreeFlow 44
KGF

KGF stands for Kolar Gold Fields.
It is located at Kolar district, Karnataka, India.
It is administered by Bharat Gold Mines Limited.
KGF is about 100 kilometers from Bangalore.
It was closed by the Indian government in 2001.
The reason of closing was environmental and economic.
Gold was found here more than 2000 years ago.
In 1880, it was controlled by British John Taylor 2nd.
Even today gold is present in this field.
Kolar got its name from Lord Kuvalala of this region.
Lord Kuvalala got the name changed as Lord Someshwara.
KGF movie based on this field was a huge success.

These are unlimited speaking topics based on interesting facts. You speak these topics in classroom limitlessly using correct accent and diction with energy and enthusiasm. These topics are also good for knowledge improvement.

FreeFlow 45
Dadasaheb Phalke

Dadasaheb Phalke is known as the father of Indian cinema.
He was born in 1870 in Nashik city of Maharashtra.
His father was an accomplished scholar of Sanskrit language.
For education, Phalke joined Sir J.J School of Art in Mumbai.
He went to Kala Bhavan in Vadodara to study drawing and painting.
He began his career as a small town photographer n Godhara.
Later he started a printing press and made his trip to Germany.
Because of a dispute he left printing and planned for motion pictures.
Dadasaheb proved successful in new art and made many silent films.
He formed a film company named Hindustan Films in Mumbai.
He made 95 movies and 26 short films in his career of 19 years.
Dadasaheb died in 1944 at the age of 73 in Nashik.
Phalke Award is for a lifetime contribution to Indian cinema.

FreeFlow 46
Lord Osho

Osho is known as the most revolutionary preacher in the world.
His real name was Chandra Mohan Jain and pet name Rajneesh.
He was named Osho because of his knowledge like an ocean.
Osho was born in 1931 at Raisen, Madhya Pradesh, India.
He did M.A in philosophy and worked for a newspaper.
He was appointed as the professor of philosophy in Jabalpur.
As an atheist, he took interest RSS, Indian Army, and hypnosis.
He had conflicts with lecturers and considered dangerous for students.
He tore out all certificates, abandoned teaching, and travelled India.
He began public speaking at annual Sarva Dharma Sammelan at Jabalpur.
Osho criticized socialism, Gandhi, and religion that made him controversial.
Osho began meditation camps and spoke openly about physical union.
First he initiated a group in Mumbai and then shifted to Pune.
He travelled to the USA and criticized openly about Christianity.
President Reagan and 21 other countries prohibited Osho's entrance.
He returned to Pune and died in 1990 after heart failure.

These are unlimited speaking topics based on interesting facts. You speak these topics in classroom limitlessly using correct accent and diction with energy and enthusiasm. These topics are also good for knowledge improvement.

FreeFlow 47
Akon

Akon is a famous Afro-American singer and music producer.
He was born in 1973 at Saint Louis, Missouri, USA.
His musician father Mor Thiam raised him in musical environment.
He learnt to play many instruments and settled in New Jersey.
His album 'Trouble' in 2004 and song 'Lonely' in 2005 got success.
The song reached the top five in US, UK, Australia, and Germany.
Next album came with 'Smack that' and Wanna love you' songs.
These two songs made Akon an international superstar.
Akon and Michael Jackson were close friends till the end.
Lady Gaga and T. Pain were given chance by Akon.
He entered Indian market after singing a song of Ra.One film.
He has his charity for supporting orphans in Africa.
Akon also owns a diamond mine in South Africa.

FreeFlow 48
Graham Bell

Graham Bell is regarded as the father of telephone.
He was born in 1847 in Edinburgh, Scotland, United Kingdom.
His father Melville Bell was a professor in a college.
Graham's wife Mabel and his mother were born deaf.
He was enrolled at Royal High School but he left education at 15.
Graham had deep interest and intelligence in phonetics.
In 1865, he was in deep experiments on sound.
He became the professor of vocal physiology at Boston University.
His entire life was to integrate the deaf with sound.
Bell realized the possibility of sending human voice over a wire.
Using transmission method he invented telephone in 1876.
Graham Bell's patent was issued by U.S Patent Office.
Graham died in 1922 at Nova Scotia in Canada.

FreeFlow 49
A.R Rahman

A.R Rahman is a renowned music director of India.
His Tamil fans affectionately call him – The Musical Storm.
His childhood name was R.S Dileep Kumar.
He was born in 1967 in a middleclass Tamil family of Chennai.
His name A.R Rahman stands for Allah Rakha Rahman.
Rahman is a famous singer, lyricist, and music director.
He follows Sufi Islam religion bestowed in him from his mother.
His parents' names are R.K Shekhar and Kareema Begum.
Rahman began his film career in 1990 with Tamil film 'Roja'.
His father R.K Shekhar was a film score composer.
Rahman assisted his father in the studio playing keyboards.
His father passed away when he was nine years old.
He learnt playing keyboard, piano, harmonium, and guitar.
At the age of eleven, he began playing in orchestra.
He's got Grammy, Academy, BAFTa Awards, and 15 Filmfare Awards.

FreeFlow 50
Volkswagen (fokswagen)

Volkswagen is a German can manufacturer.
It has headquarter is at Lower Saxony, Germany.
This company has more than 6 lakhs workers worldwide.
It was founded by German Labor Front in the year of 1937.
German Labor Front was the labor organization of the Nazi Party.
Volkswagen is the largest car maker company worldwide.
Its biggest market is China that delivers 40% profit.
In German, Volks means 'people', and wagen means 'car'.
This company has close competition with Toyota of Japan.
Volkswagen also owns Audi and Lamborghini car companies.
Volkswagen vehicles are well equipped and safe.
It has plenty of intelligent technology for safety.
Volkswagen sold around three million cars in 2021.

These are unlimited speaking topics based on interesting facts. You speak these topics in classroom limitlessly using correct accent and diction with energy and enthusiasm. These topics are also good for knowledge improvement.

FreeFlow 51
Monica Lewinsky

Monica is considered the most scandalous lady of America.
She was born in 1973 in San Francisco, California.
She is a television personality and fashion designer.
Monica was a White House intern in the government of Bill Clinton.
Her father is a doctor and mother is an author.
Lewinsky graduated in psychology from Pacific Hills College.
She started her first work in drama department of her college.
Monica developed her first affair with her instructor.
From family connection, she got a job in the White House.
Monica developed her relation with President Bill Clinton.
This scandal led to President Clinton's impeachment.
As a result of the public coverage, Monica got the celebrity status.

Spicy Notions

Interesting concepts good for developing speech.
Highly effective to attract audience.
You can make short changes if required.
In speaking in classroom, apply energy and enthusiasm.
Use correct pronunciation and good accent and diction.

Concept 1
Foundation of Cambridge

Cambridge is one of the most famous universities of the world. The start of Cambridge University is taken as 1209, when scholars from Oxford migrated to Cambridge to escape Oxford's violence between townpeople and scholars. To avert possible troubles, the authorities in Cambridge allowed only scholars under the supervision of a master to remain in the town. It was partly to provide an orderly place of residence. The first college, Peterhouse, was founded in 1284 by Hugo de Balsham, bishop of Ely. Over the next three centuries another 15 colleges were founded, and after three decades Cambridge received formal recognition from Pope John XXII. Cambridge remained fairly insignificant until about 1502, when a professorship of divinity was founded. In 1546 Henry VIII founded Trinity College which still remains the largest of the Cambridge colleges. In 1570 Elizabeth I gave the university a revised body of statutes, and the university was formally incorporated by act of Parliament. Isaac Newton held the chair for over 30 years and gave the study of mathematics a unique position in the university. The famous alumni of Cambridge are Charles Darwin, Stephen Hawking, Jawaharlal Nehru and Dr. Manmohan Singh.

Concept 2
History of Australia

The first fleet of British ships arrived at Botany Bay in Sydney in January 1788. The purpose of this fleet was to establish a penal colony, the first colony on the Australian mainland. In the century that followed, the British established other colonies on the continent, and European explorers ventured into its interior. Aboriginal people were greatly weakened and their numbers diminished by introduced diseases and conflict with the colonists during this period. Gold rushes and agricultural industries brought prosperity. Transportation of British convicts to Australia was phased out from 1840 to 1868. Autonomous parliamentary democracies began to be established throughout the six British colonies from the mid-19th century. The colonies voted by referendum to unite in a federation in 1901, and modern Australia came into being. Australia fought as part of British Empire and later Commonwealth in the two world wars and was to become a long-standing ally of the United States when threatened by Imperial Japan during World War II. Trade with Asia increased and a post-war immigration program received more than 6.5 million migrants from every continent. Supported by immigration of people from almost every country in the world since the end of World War II, the population increased to more than 25.5 million by 2020, with 30 per cent of the population born overseas.

Concept 3
Invention of Internet

Computer science was an emerging discipline in the late 1950s. Early fixed-program computers in the 1940s were operated manually by entering small programs via switches in order to load and run a series of programs. As transistor technology evolved in the 1950s, central processing units and user terminals came into use and the mainframe computer model was devised. In the early age, computers had largely been used only as mathematical devices. In the late 1960s, with the creation of a company named Advanced Research Projects Agency Network (ARPANET), which was funded by the U.S. Department of Defense, the first workable prototype of the Internet was born. With ARPANET multiple computers were able to communicate with one another on a single network. ARPANET delivered its first message on October 29, 1969, from one computer located at the University of California Los Angeles to another at Stanford. As technology advanced, by 1970s with the work of two scientists, Robert Kahn and Vint Cerf who developed a communications model, standardizing how data was transmitted in multiple networks. Their method was adopted by ARPANET in 1983, and this is how modern internet was born proclaiming Vint Cerf as the father of internet.

Concept 4
Origin of Hip hip Hooray

Hip hip hooray is a cheer called out to express congratulation toward someone. The call was recorded in England in the beginning of the 19th century in connection with making a toast. In this sentence, the word 'hip' is a Latin acronym of "Hierosolyma Est Perdita". It means "Jerusalem is lost". This term gained notoriety in the German 'Hep hep riots' of 1819. This violence was orchestrated against Jews in Bavaria state of Germany. Saying 'Jerusalem is lost' was to disgrace Jews in Christian world. Later Nazis used this phrase to round up Jews during the Holocaust. During this period, Jewish expansion was largely hated by Christians. Even before Christians, Romans too hated Jews because religious rivalry in the region of Eurasia. The Romans have expelled the majority of Jews in 70 CE. Since then the Jewish people have always been present in the land of Israel. These days, it is advised by tourist guides to not speak 'Hip hip hooray' in Israel as it may aggravate them.

Concept 5
United Kingdom

United Kingdom is an integrated sovereign country. It is made up of four countries; England, Scotland, Wales and Northern Ireland. England accounts for 53 percent of area of the United Kingdom. The first inhabitants of England were the Celtic tribes in Iron Age. And the entire island what is UK now was called 'Pritani' island. After Julius Caesar's expeditions, the Romans began a serious and sustained attempt to conquer Pritani in the year 43 CE. In the 5th century, there lived some tribes in Anglia peninsula of northern Germany. Upon reaching a new land in Pritani, these tribes coming from Anglia, named themselves Angle. And subsequently, the land they had occupied got named as Angle – land, which later became England. Gradually Pritani got furbished as Britannia, and then Britain. The Angle tribes used German as their language. But in 12th century, France invaded England and French also became the language of England. From 13th century, the dual inhabitants of England started working upon developing their own language on the grounds of German and French. Geoffrey Chaucer, a Frenchman living in England during 14th century is regarded as the father of English literature. In the year of 1453 English people got victory over the French.

Concept 6
Who Are Americans?

In olden days, America was the land of Navajo tribe and Maya tribe until 14th century. Columbus, an Italian explorer and navigator reached America in search of India in 15th century. After him, Amerigo Vespucci, the next Italian explorer discovered America and give his name. Spain was the first of the European countries to colonize this New World. People from France, England, Netherlands, and Sweden did not settle in the Americas until after 1600. By the expansion of Europeans, the Navajo and Maya tribes got widely downsized. Now the United States constitute the majority of Europeans which is around 58%, then 14 percent Africans, and 7% Asians. The 2022 American Community Survey found these top reported European ancestries in the U.S. as: English people 20%, German 19%, Spanish 19%, and Italian 7%. The Navajo and Maya tribe, now called the Native Americans, widely shrunk down by population live as minority in the United States of America. The original Mayans, shifting towards Latin America have had Guatemala as their own county.

Concept 7
Sunday As Holiday

Initially, Christianity had Saturday as holiday following the principle of Judaism. When Christian doctrine spread widely, the sun worshiper pagans of Eurasia were the next to convert into Christianity. The pagans put a condition that their sun-day should be considered as the holy-day in Christianity. As the condition was accepted, in 321 CE, it was Emperor Constantine who decreed that the seven-day week was the official Roman week and made 'Sunday' a public holiday. He introduced the first civil legislation concerning Sunday and commanded that all work should cease on this day, except that farmers could work, if necessary. Besides 'Sunday' as a holiday, the Romans also wanted 'Saturday' to be considered as half-day, as Saturday was the 'Sabbath' among the Jews and the only day named after a Roman God - Saturn. In support of this historical belief, most employers in the modern world, consider giving their employees a half-day on a Saturday.

Concept 8
Invention of Motion Picture

The human eye and brain can process a maximum of about 12 still images per second. If more than 12 still images run in a second, human brain misunderstand them to be moving. Louis Le Prince, a French artist and inventor took this misunderstanding as the source of invention. He thought about a camouflage of running 30 still images (frames) per second — technically called 30 fps. He created a two second video named 'Roundhay Garden Scene', a short silent motion picture in England in 1888. This motion picture had 52 frames that ran in two seconds at the speed to 24 fps. It as a remarkable display of 4 people walking in a garden. This motion picture was watched in Kinetoscope, an early motion picture exhibition device. And this way, Louis Le Prince takes the credit of being the father of motion picture. After him, John Logie Baird, a Scottish inventor living in the UK invented a video camera in 1925.

Concept 9
Is Moon Habitable?

Oxygen required for breathing is not present on moon's atmosphere. So, humans cannot breathe on the Moon. The lunar environment presents unique challenges. Though solar energy is also available on the moon but the lunar night is exponentially colder and longer than the night here on the earth. Because of the moon's sparse atmosphere, there is no protection from meteorites or radiation. The temperature fluctuations on the moon are also intense, ranging from -248 to 123 degrees Celsius. To make the moon habitable, we would need to live in shelters. In addition to protecting us from meteorites, radiation and toxic lunar dust, a sealed shelter would allow us to breathe. Taking a breath on the moon would be deadly. The moon technically does have an atmosphere, but the gases are so spread out that they aren't much help for breathing. So, we'll need a reliable and renewable energy supply. Although NASA is developing power generation systems that could support longer stays on the lunar surface, additional energy infrastructure will be needed to make human settlement on the moon a reality.

Concept 10
How Cricket Started?

The word 'cricket' is originated from 'crackle' which means - To make a rapid succession of short sharp noises. Cricket is believed to have begun in 13th century in England as a game. The country boys would bowl at a tree stump or at the hurdle gate into a sheep pen using a stone ball. The primitive bat was no doubt a shaped branch of a tree, resembling a modern hockey stick but considerably longer and heavier. The change to a straight bat was made to defend against length bowling, which had evolved with cricketers in Hambledon, a small village in southern England. The aforementioned Hambledon Club, playing in Hampshire, was the predominant cricket force in the second half of the 18th century before the rise of the Marylebone Cricket Club in London. Moving to the current ground in St. John's Wood in 1814, Lord's became the headquarters of world cricket. In 1836 the first match of North counties versus South counties was played, providing clear evidence of the spread of cricket. It became an established sport in the country in the 18th century and developed globally in the 19th and 20th centuries. William Gilbert Grace, a British schoolboy athlete, is considered the father of cricket. In cricket career, he scored 54,896 runs and registered 126 centuries.

Concept 11
Why doesn't Putin move his right hand while walking?

Russian President Vladimir Putin was the Soviet KGB agent before acquiring presidency. KGB was a foreign intelligence and domestic security agency of the Soviet Union. As an intelligence agent, Putin received intense weapon training and rose to the rank of lieutenant colonel. As per the training manual he had to hold weapons in right hand while walking. This developed Gunslinger's gait, a distinct style of walking in Putin. The KGB manual describes the perfect way how a KGB officer should walk, in order to handle weapons at any time. According to the KGB manual, its operatives are instructed to keep their weapon in their right hand close to their chest and to move forward with one side, usually the left, presumably allowing subjects to draw the gun as quickly as possible when confronted with an enemy.

Concept 12
Why do computers have C and D drive, not A or B?

It's because A and B drive was used as floppy drives since beginning in computers. Decades ago floppy drives were the norm and there was no hard disk. The letter C was given to any hard disk that the user installed. The drives A and B have since then been reserved for floppy drives. Unsurprisingly, the answer lies in Microsoft's DOS operating system. Long before Windows existed, most PC-compatible computer systems had only one disk drive in it - a floppy disk drive. At the time, users would insert their DOS floppy disk into the computer just before they turned it on, and the computer would start, or "boot up" via the software on the floppy. As the first and often only disk drive installed in the computer, the floppy disk was assigned the first letter of the alphabet as – A drive.

Concept 13
What is the use of the fifth small pocket in jeans pants?

The denim fabric was created in Nimes city of France during 1800. Jeans were originally created as practical work wear, and their indigo color was chosen so that it would better hide the dirt when worn by miners and laborers. And it was in 1873, in the USA, in San Francisco, that Davis & Levi Strauss made the first 5-pocket jeans that you know today. This innovation of jeans created the garment so strong that it came to clothe nearly all American laborers by the 1930. Measuring 5 cm wide, it's stitched into the right front pocket. It was originally designed to accommodate the pocket watch, round and flat that slipped in perfectly. It was a very useful and almost essential accessory of the time. This is why it was also called the watch pocket.

Concept 14
What does Rx mean on a medical prescription?

The "Rx" symbol is commonly known as the symbol for a medical prescription. In olden days, Rome using Latin language, had to write "to take" for a prescription. And the word "to take" in Latin is – "recipere". In order to shorten this word, they picked up 'R' and added extra 'x' to create a symbol of– Rx. This Rx symbol evolved from the Eye of Horus, an ancient Egyptian symbol associated with healing powers. The Eye of Horus, a powerful symbol associated with protection and healing was used in medicinal and protective contexts. This symbol is often depicted as a stylized human eye with markings. Romans culturally associated with Egyptians designed Rx as per the Eye of Horus.

Concept 15
Why is it called Dead Sea in southwestern Asia?

First of all, despite its name, the Dead Sea is not a sea but just a lake. It is a hypersaline (too salty) lake landlocked between Israel and Jordan in southwestern Asia. Its eastern shore belongs to Jordan, and the southern half to Israel. Its Arabic name is "albahr almayit" which literally means "Sea Dead". It is called the Dead Sea because no life such as plants or living creatures could survive in its waters, although it does contain some microbial life. The water full of salt makes it much denser and heavier than freshwater. So if you swim in it, you float very easily. It temporarily comes to life in the wake of rainy winters. Its salt production has been used to treat various skin conditions.

Concept 16
Why Abdul Rashid Khan changed his name as Shahrukh Khan?

Shahrukh Khan's real name is Abdul Rashid Khan. Born in New Delhi, he spent the first five years of his life in Mangalore, where his maternal grandfather, Iftikhar Ahmed, served as chief engineer of the port. Khan attended St. Columba's School in central Delhi where he excelled in his studies and in sports such as hockey and football. Initially Khan aspired to pursue a career in sports, however owing to a shoulder injury in his early years meant that he could no longer play. Instead, in his youth, he acted in stage plays and received praise. Khan's first starring role was in a television series Dil Dariya, which began shooting in 1988, but production delays led to 1989 series Fauji becoming his television debut instead. This was the time when his elder sister Shehnaz got married to Lalarukh Khan. Looking for a good screen name, inspired from Lalarukh, he changed his name as Shahrukh Khan.

Concept 17
Why Shivaji Rao Gaikwad chose to become Rajinikanth?

Rajinikanth was born as Shivaji Rao Gaikwad in a Marathi Hindu family in Bangalore. His brother enrolled him at the Ramakrishna Matth, a Hindu monastery set up by the Ramakrishna Mission. In the matth, he was taught Vedas, tradition and history, which eventually instilled a sense of spirituality in him. In addition to spiritual lessons, he also began acting in plays at the matth. His aspiration towards theatre grew from there. Upon completion of his school education, Rajinikanth performed several jobs including that of a coolie, before getting a job in the Bangalore Transport Service as a bus conductor. He continued to take part in plays and decided to take up an acting course in Madras Film Institute. During his stay at the institute, he was noticed by the Tamil film director K. Balachander who provided him with his stage name Rajinikanth to avoid confusion with fellow actor Sivaji Ganesan, having taken it from a character's name in his earlier film Major Chandrakanth.

Concept 18
Why do pirates wear an eye patch?

There is an interesting perspective about why the pirates wear an eye patch. It's not to hide their missing or injured eye but to condition the eye for fighting in darkness. A pirate's life at sea is hard. You may know this that the lower decks of a ship at sea are dark while the upper decks are very bright — especially because of the light reflecting off the water. The challenge here is that it takes 20–30 minutes for the human eye to fully adapt from bright sunlight to seeing in complete darkness. Now, if a pirate was fighting on the upper deck in the sunlight, then had to continue the fight under in the lower deck where it is usually pretty dark, it could take too long for their eyes to adjust, allowing him to see. The eye-patch used to help in preparing one eye to see in the dark, so when they would go to the lower deck pirates could swap the eye patch from one eye to the other and see with the eye that has already adjusted to dim light. This would help them to instantly see in the dark.

Concept 19
Why does honey never spoil?

Honey can stay edible for years and decades. It is a natural product which means it will change in color and taste over time but will never get spoilt. For honey, those changes may include darkening color, thicker consistency, and different taste. Changes in honey are good signs proving the product is high quality and unpasteurized. Honey is naturally antimicrobial, so it has been used throughout history for health improvement. Honey's low moisture doesn't allow bacteria to survive. And without bacteria, honey just doesn't spoil. What's more, the bees add their own enzymes to honey, and these enzymes produce hydrogen peroxide - the antiseptic element.

Concept 20
Is the portrait of Mona Lisa a man or a woman?

Mona Lisa is an imaginary portrait painting by Italian artist Leonardo da Vinci. From five centuries, the portrait hangs behind bulletproof glass within the Louvre Museum of Paris and draws thousands of jostling spectators each day. Born in a religiously nondenominational family, inspired from Mother Mary, Leonardo wanted to draw a unique painting. Looking into polytheistic Kemetism religion of Egypt, he studied about God Amon and Goddess Lisa designated as the deities of love. Merging these two characters in one, and creating the word Mona Lisa out of "Amon + Lisa", he drew the painting which became universally famous over time.

Cromosys
Education and Technology Research Center

Spoken English Topics

+91-9561450045
Nallasopara (W), Mumbai
www.facebook.com/cromosys

NIRANJAN JHA SHOWMAN

Founder - Niranjan Jha Showman

Education and Technology Research Center

Patankar Park, Nallasopara (W), Mumbai. +91-9561450045

Education, Technology, Publication, Healthcare, Newsmedia, Realtor, Filmmaking

www.facebook.com/cromosys

Cromosys Publication
Teach
Yourself
German
NIRANJAN JHA SHOWMAN

Cromosys Publication
Teach
Yourself
French
NIRANJAN JHA SHOWMAN

Cromosys Publication
Teach
Yourself
Spanish
NIRANJAN JHA SHOWMAN

Cromosys Publication

English Voice Accent and Pronunciation

NIRANJAN JHA SHOWMAN

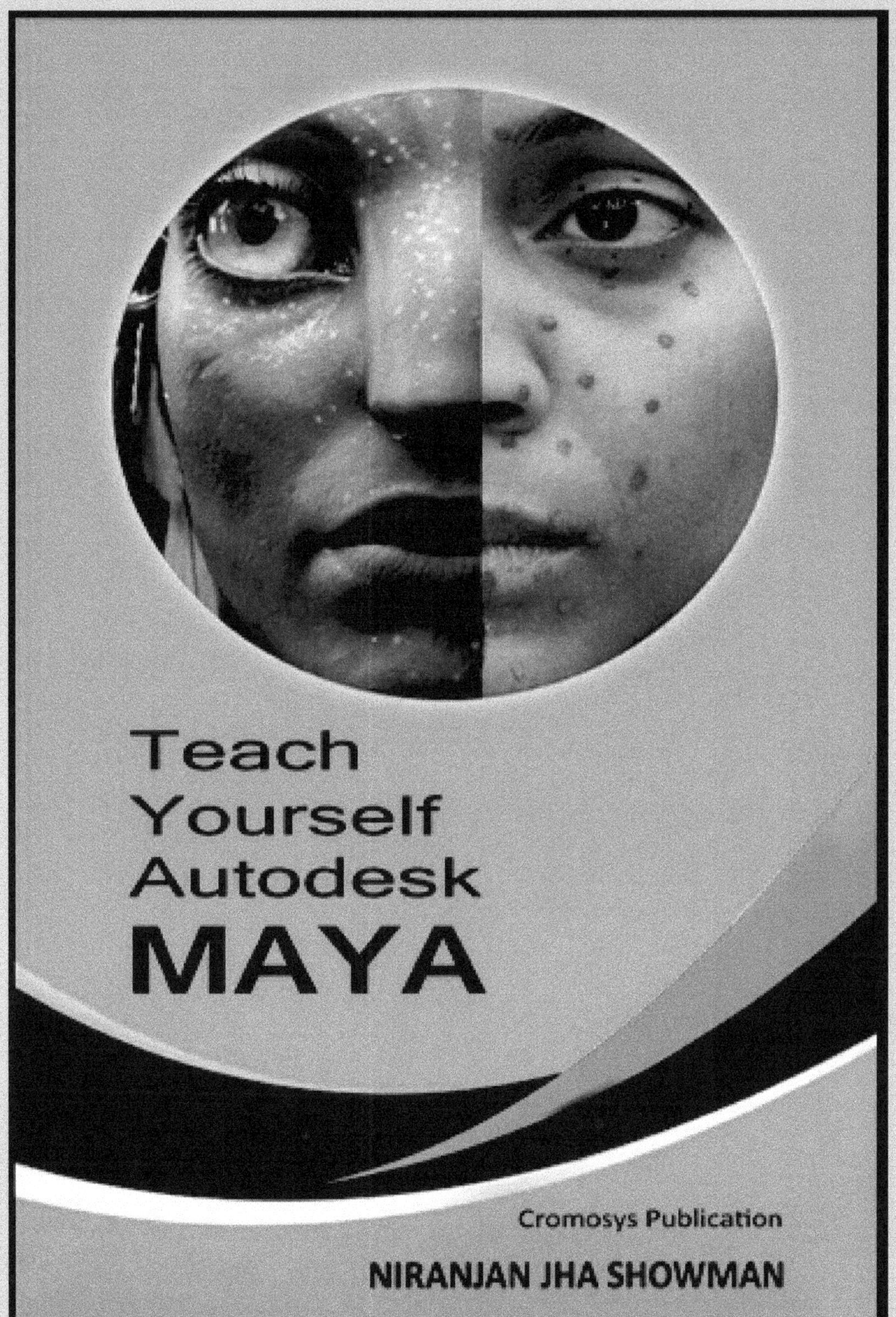

Teach
Yourself
Autodesk
MAYA
Cromosys Publication
NIRANJAN JHA SHOWMAN

Cromosys Publication
Teach
Yourself
Autodesk
3ds Max
NIRANJAN JHA SHOWMAN

Cromosys Publication
CRIMINAL FACTORY
NIRANJAN JHA SHOWMAN

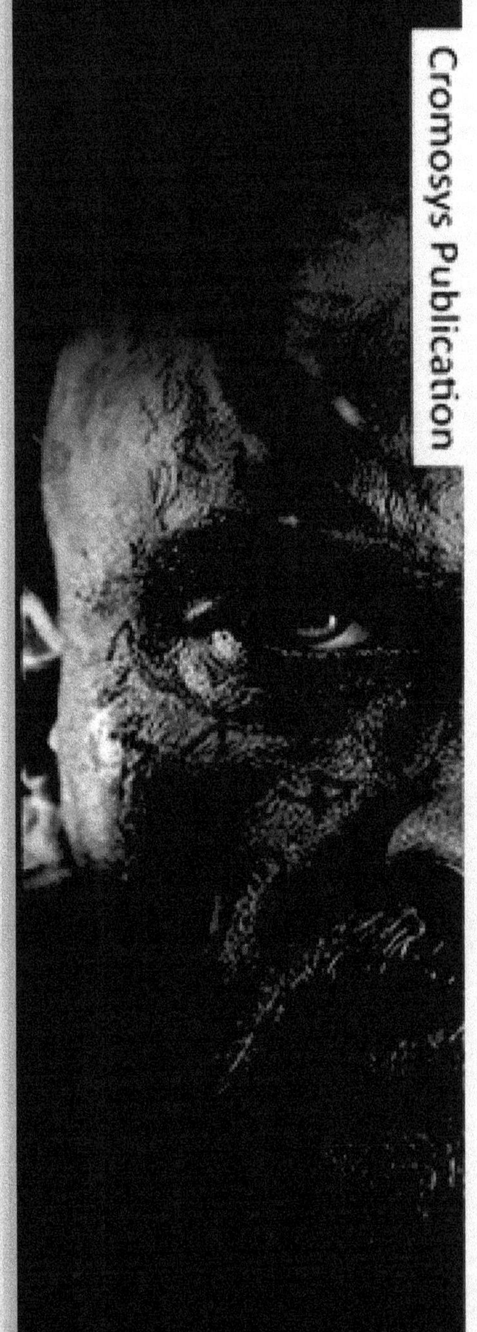

Cromosys Publication
FOCAL DISASTER
NIRANJAN JHA SHOWMAN

Cromosys Publication
Your talents will not help you succeed without your skill of using them.
NIRANJAN JHA SHOWMAN
BE
MILLIONAIRE
LIKE
ME

Copyright Office
Government of India

सत्यमेव जयते

Extracts
from the Register
of Copyrights

Dated : 16/08/2022

1.	Registration Number	:	**T-96784-2022**
2.	Name, address and nationality of the applicant	:	NIRANJAN JHA SHOWMAN, CROMOSYS PUBLICATION, 001, JAYSATYAM, PATANKAR ROAD, NALLASOPARA (W), MUMBAI, MAHARASHTRA - 401203. INDIAN
3.	Nature of the applicant's interest in the copyright of the work	:	AUTHOR
4.	Class and description of the work	:	LITERARY / BOOK
5.	Title of the work	:	**SPOKEN ENGLISH TOPICS**
6.	Language of the work	:	ENGLISH
7.	Name, address and nationality of the author and if the author is deceased, date of his decease	:	NIRANJAN JHA SHOWMAN, CROMOSYS PUBLICATION, 001, JAYSATYAM, PATANKAR ROAD, NALLASOPARA (W), MUMBAI, MAHARASHTRA - 401203. INDIAN
8.	Whether the work is published or unpublished	:	UNPUBLISHED
9.	Year and country of first publication and name, address and nationality of the publisher	:	N.A.
10.	Years and countries of subsequent publications, if any, and names, addresses and nationalities of the publishers	:	N.A. SAME AS ABOVE
11.	Names, addresses and nationalities of the owners of various rights comprising the copyright in the work and the extent of rights held by each, together with particulars of assignments and licences, if any	:	
12.	Names, addresses and nationalities of other persons, if any, authorised to assign or licence of rights comprising the copyright	:	N.A.
13.	If the work is an 'Artistic work', the location of the original work, including name, address and nationality of the person in possession of the work. (In the case of an architectural work, the year of completion of the work should also be shown).	:	N.A.
14.	If the work is an 'Artistic work', whether it is registered under the Designs Act 2000 if yes give details.	:	N.A.
15.	If the work is an 'Artistic work', capable of being registered as a design under the Designs Act 2000.whether it has been applied to an article though an industrial process and ,if yes ,the number of times it is reproduced.	:	N.A.
16.	Remarks, if any	:	

Diary Number : 9424/2022-DF/T
Date of Application : 25/08/2022
Date of Receipt : 25/08/2022

DEPUTY REGISTRAR OF COPYRIGHTS